MPOWER ME

MPOWER ME

The 3-part Combination to Shift from Struggle to a Life of Significance, Strength, and Success

Roger L. Daye

Unless otherwise marked, all scripture quotations taken from The Holy Bible, King James Version. Cambridge Edition: 1769; King James Bible Online, 2018. www.kingjamesbibleonline.org.

Scripture quotations marked TLB taken from The Living Bible copyright © 1971. Used by permission of Tyndale House Publishers, Inc., Carol Stream, Illinois 60188. All rights reserved.

Scripture quotations marked NASB taken from the New American Standard Bible. La Habra, CA: Foundation Publications, for the Lockman Foundation, 1971. Print.

Scripture quotations marked (NIrV) are taken from the Holy Bible, New International Reader's Version®, NIrV®. Copyright © 1995, 1996, 1998, 2014 by Biblica, Inc.™ Used by permission of Zondervan. All rights reserved worldwide.

"NIrV" and "New International Reader's Version" are trademarks registered in the United States Patent and Trademark Office by Biblica, Inc.™

Scripture quotations marked MSG taken from the Holy Bible: The Message (the Bible in contemporary language). 2005. Colorado Springs, CO: NavPress.

Paperback ISBN: 978-1-968250-59-1
Hardcover ISBN: 978-1-968250-60-7
Digital ISBN: 978-1-968250-61-4

GC GAME CHANGER PUBLISHING
www.GameChangerPublishing.com

I dedicate this book to my children,

MeCaiah and DeVante'

If love were money, I would be the wealthiest man in the world.

Read This First

Just to say Thank You, I would like

to give you a Free Gift!

Scan the QR Code:

SCAN ME for a FREE GIFT

ACKNOWLEDGMENTS

I want to acknowledge everyone at **Game Changer Publishing**
who contributed to helping me make this book a reality.

Words cannot express my gratitude, thanks, and appreciation for your
genius, creativity, and passionate care for this endeavor.

Your dedication to excellence shows what God
can do with just a "few folks."

"These are they that turn the world upside down."
— *Acts 17:6*

ADVANCE PRAISE

"MPOWER ME is a timely message to today's Christian community. As we watch the dark clouds of purposelessness and mediocrity creep across the skies of our society, it has never been more important than now for God's people to obtain the combination shared in this book to unlock their potential and fulfill their Kingdom purpose in this age."
— **John Shaw**, Small Group Leader, Berean Christian Church

"This book will give you the direction and guidance needed to take a meaningful step in the right direction—whether it's in your business or the goals you are setting in life. I love the references to scripture and the easy-to-follow steps in the book."
— **Natalia L.**

"Mr. Daye has done a tremendous amount of research on what it takes to be successful, based on biblical principles as well as relevant and pertinent business concepts. Anyone reading MPOWER ME should be able to take that first important step toward whatever they are striving to do and 'master' their way to accomplishment and success!"
— **Barbara Lipscomb**

"This book is an engaging piece of material, encouraging all its readers to set aside disabling mindsets, adopt God's vision and plan for their lives, and boldly obtain wealth and thrive using His Spirit. So rich... (no pun intended)."
— **Yvonne J.**

"This book, MPOWER ME, has given me encouragement to get up and move! Stop looking at my neighbor and see what God has planned specifically for me with my spiritual gift. The positive affirmations reinforce that I must change my thinking to change my direction."
— **Debra R. Dice**

"MPOWER ME gave me encouragement, guidance, and tools to self-evaluate my situation and grow spiritually and financially."

— **Minister Tabatha Doby**

"No more excuses! The combination to success is no longer a mystery. MPOWER ME encourages the reader to make a valuable paradigm shift and, from there, to launch into the deep. This is the book for dreamers who need a little push."

— **Wilveria K. Shaw**

"I recommend MPOWER as a guide to follow for success. This book offers an array of vital Golden Nuggets (valuable information). MPOWER offers powerful info that guarantees attainable success. This is an Amazingly Awesome roadmap; thank you Roger Daye for sharing your God inspired wisdom with us."

— **Pamela Curry**

MPOWER ME

The 3-part Combination
to Shift from Struggle to a Life of
Significance, Strength, and Success

Roger L. Daye

FOREWORD

It is not often that a book comes along that is a relevant, well-written piece of art that speaks to the reader on so many different levels, while offering sound and thought-provoking conversation, and has the potential to change lives. Simply put, *MPOWER ME* is *that* book.

MPOWER ME is a masterpiece yet to be discovered. It is just a matter of time before the masses recognize its wisdom, understanding, and knowledge.

Reading Roger Daye's work is like talking to an old friend, one who listens and understands your dilemma, but in the next breath delivers a ray of truth to challenge your thoughts and bring you back into reality. As I read it, I found myself interacting with Roger, crying at times, laughing out loud, and even pausing to fall on my knees and pray. Yes, it is *that* kind of read. I was struck by the profound yet simple and easy-to-read approach. Pure gold, each chapter is anointed to complete what it is destined to do and change the lives it has been appointed to change.

Common sense combined with pure genius, the work encourages the reader to dream bigger, recognize who they are, stop procrastinating, and take action. Chock full of step-by-step instructions and wise counsel, "*MPOWER*" will move you from where you are to where you want to be. "*MPOWER*" is not just a book—but it is a wake-up call, a blueprint, a rule manual, a play book, a how-to guide, and a coaching session all in one.

As I read it, I was struck with an overwhelming gratitude that I was the first one to read something so profoundly monumental—a vision destined to help millions of people find their way.

I was challenged, called out, rebuked, and encouraged. I found myself in a conversation with this book. "*MPOWER*" will challenge you too, to walk in your God given purpose and authority in ways for which you may not be ready. With that thought, I encourage you to remain vigilant; do not stop reading even when the message is hard to hear and calls out your particular problem, habit, or issue. It will bring to light the reality of that uneasy feeling often in the back of our minds—a knowing that we should be in service to others that God has put in our lives.

I became increasingly grateful for the opportunity to read this work because, as I read, my thoughts were moved to a higher frequency. Again, I say to you, remain patient and persistent, because you have much to gain from this work.

Leaders will want to read it with their teams and share it with church and business groups. "*MPOWER ME*" is for the young person just starting as much as it is for the seasoned baby Boomer who feels they may have missed the window of opportunity.

Again, "*MPOWER ME*" *is that book.* It will join the many great books in my library that I often refer to for myself and recommend to friends, colleagues, and young people alike.

Karen Maxfield-Lunkin, Ph.D.
Bridgeucation Creative Education Consultants

Table of Contents

Disclaimer

There are some great authors who write their magnum opus, as the "be all, end all" of their genius, but this book is not intended to be a literary masterpiece. Truthfully, this is a conglomeration of thoughts, ideas, and concepts I have amassed over the years through some tough life lessons that caused me a lot of headaches and heartaches. I am sharing this with you in the hopes that it blesses you in some capacity, so that you can apply it and see fruitfulness from it. History will tell what impact this piece of work will have had.

At first glance, you may think this is a random collection of strange thoughts and hard-to-prove theories, but it is not. Some parts of the Book may seem fragmented or not have the flow that you would expect.

I ask you to do me the simple favor of not "starting, then stopping" before you make any final judgment as to whether this book is good or bad; please read it from beginning to end. Although you may not initially understand the method to my madness, I promise your "stick-to-itiveness" will pay off.

The best example of what I mean by the paragraph above is when you look at the back of a tapestry: it looks like a confusing mess, but by the time you turn it around (when you finish the book) you will see a wonderfully strategic and beautifully interwoven pattern; a picture of your most successful self.

I have tried to express what God gave me to share with you in excellence, although you may not agree with everything that I say, and that is fine.

We can agree to disagree, but hopefully, you at least get the gist of what I am trying to say. I pray to God that this will be enough to compel you to action.

I have one ultimate goal with this book: to give you a comprehensive means of using your "power to get wealth" (Deuteronomy 8:18).

However, wealth in this context means more than "mere" money. It is wealth in its truest essence, which is Strength, Significance, and Success.

The three areas where you want to be most wealthy are in your Life, Leadership, and Legacy.

I will clearly explain (in this book) how to make this happen for you, but for now, I will simply say you must allow God to **"MPOWER"** You!

Preface

Wealth comes through intentional effort to the right person, but it often eludes those who put in blood, sweat, and tears, yet they are the wrong person. Have you ever wondered to yourself, "If something is wrong with me," you know you are doing the hard work, but you do not get the results you desire. Beloved, we need to understand what it means to be the right person.

T. Harv Eker said in his book, *Secrets of the Millionaire Mind*, "It is not about being in the right place at the right time, it is about being the *right person* in the right place at the right time."[1]

I know what it feels like to be the wrong person, and I know what it takes to become the right person. Are "YOU" ready to learn how to be the right person?

PURITY LEADS TO PROSPERITY

"But they that seek the Lord shall not want any good thing."
— Psalm 34:10b

"For the Lord God is a sun and shield:
the Lord will give grace and glory:
no good thing will he withhold from them that walk uprightly."
— Psalm 84:11

---

[1] Eker, T. Harv, Secrets of the Millionaire Mind (New York City: HarperCollins Publishers, 2009); page 9

In the Kingdom of God, you must be "right" to receive. I am not talking about right as in "correct," but right as in *"righteous."* People have defined righteousness in different ways, but the simplest definition of *righteousness* for our discussion is "one who is in right standing with God." According to the scriptures mentioned above, there is nothing necessary for success that God will not "release to the righteous." Talking right, walking right, living right—this is what it means to be righteous. Does this describe you? Because if it does, there is no "good thing" that God will withhold from you.

If you think you are unworthy of the description above, then you may also feel unqualified and ready to put down the book. DON'T!

Again, let me assure you, I was once the wrong person, but I have learned what it takes to become the "right" person. And for you to achieve that, all you need to do is commit to the process.

Notice, I did not say you have to be "perfect" to receive. *Righteous* does not mean perfect. It does not even mean you do everything 100% right, and never make a mistake. On the contrary, it means that you ALWAYS give 100% to make things right with God when you make a mistake.

So, how do you make things right with God, you ask? Simple, LEARN from it! God does not expect perfection; He expects maturity. And a sign of maturity is not to keep repeating the same mistakes over and over. Making mistakes is inevitable, but this is not what's holding you back. Making the same mistakes repeatedly in different situations is what's hindering your progress and keeping you stuck.

> *"For a just man falleth seven times, and riseth up again."*
> **— Proverbs 24:16a**

What makes the man "just" if he keeps "falling"?

The answer is: his ability to rise up again.

Let's break down this scripture: the word "just" here means righteous, "falling" means mistakes (or to fail), and "rise" means to establish, or better yet, to re-establish. When you put those words together, you can see that the man's righteousness (or how he stays in right standing with God) *after he makes a mistake* is his capacity to reestablish himself in God.

How do you "reestablish" yourself *in God*? Well, it is a three-fold process:

Repent, Renew, Results.

❖ Repent. This shows God you recognize you made a mistake and you want to change for the better.

❖ Renew your mind. We will talk more about this in Chapter 6. For now, just understand that, according to Romans 12:2, the catalyst for your transformation begins with your mind.

❖ Results. This shows God that you have reestablished (Proverbs 24:16a) yourself when He sees productivity in your life.

KNOWING WHAT TO DO VERSUS DOING WHAT YOU KNOW

The biggest roadblock you will face as you read this book and learn how to receive what God has for you is *what you already know*. We often say things like, "I already know that." But the issue is not *knowing what to do*. It is *doing what you know*. Let's be honest, YOU "MAY" KNOW IT, BUT ARE YOU DOING IT? "Knowledge is Power" is a cliché, but knowing (in and of itself) is not power; it is what you do with what you know that is *true* power.

> *"Knowing is not enough; we must apply.*
> *Willing is not enough; we must do."*
> **— Bruce Lee**

APPLICATION IS ALWAYS BETTER THAN REVELATION

"It is better to know little and DO it all
than to know it all and do little."
— **Roger L. Daye**
(My interpretation of James 1:22)

You must develop the "Discipline of Doing." This is a concept you will become thoroughly acquainted with as you read this book. So, as we embark on this quest for greatness, the first thing you must do is get out of your own way. Forget what you already know; please EMPTY YOUR CUP as I challenge "YOU" to change, because you cannot fill a cup that is already full. Biblically put, it is as Jesus said in *Matthew 9:17*, *"No man puts new wine into old bottles."* To say it plainly:

"You can't put new ideas into old mindsets.
You can't get new results with old behaviors."
— **Reverend Wayne Manning**

RINSE AND REPEAT

While reading, you will see I have purposely created "consistency through redundancy" by intentionally repeating certain scriptures, quotes, and important concepts specific to this philosophy. This was done because one of the best ways to learn is via repetitive information to make it stick. The Bible says, *"Faith cometh by hearing and hearing by the Word of God" (Romans 10:17)*. Put differently, that means revelation is reinforced through repetition. The continual rehearsing of the same (or a similar) thing being consistently heard, spoken, and thought about will build your faith in any area.

CHOICES CREATE CIRCUMSTANCES

Tony Robbins once said,

> *"What is the single force that shapes the quality of our lives? What power do we have that can change everything? As you and I both know, the answer is the power of CHOICE."*[2]

Choice is defined as the opportunity or power to choose between two or more possibilities; the opportunity or power to decide. Here is the truth we sometimes do not like to admit: the quality of our lives depends upon the quality of our choices.

Tony Robbins went on to say,

> ***"It is our choices, not our conditions, which determine the quality of our lives.*** *Before we go any further, we need to understand we are where we are today because of the decisions we've made—decisions about what to focus on, decisions about where to place our priorities, decisions about what things mean, and decisions about what to do."*

DECISIONS DICTATE DESTINY

I am asking that you make a "destiny decision" right now. Commit yourself to reading this book with an open mind, an open heart, and an open spirit, then allow God to do the rest. God gave you the power to get wealth. If you don't have it, then it is your fault. This may sound harsh and insensitive, but sometimes the truth is a bitter pill that must be swallowed. And sometimes being forced to swallow that bitter pill is what brings us to the place in life where we say, "Enough is Enough!" At that point, we decide within ourselves that we will break the cycle that has perpetuated failure and non-

---

[2] Robbins, Tony. Business Thought. Profit Magazin, 2008.
www.profitmagazin.com/editions/number_061.481.html

accomplishment in our lives. In this moment, we realize that if things are ever going to change, then we will have to change them.

Beloved, it is my firm conviction that you are at that place right now, and the book you are holding is the first step in the direction of a better you. Be the change you desire to see, and there is nothing that can stop you, other than you.

MPOWER ME

INTRODUCTION
The Power To Get Wealth

POOR
Never Having Enough

"For the poor shall never cease out of the land."
— Deuteronomy 15:11

RICH
Having Too Much

"Behold, these are the ungodly,
who prosper in the world;
they increase in riches."
— Psalm 73:12

WEALTH
Having More Than Enough

"…God is able to give you more than you need,
so that you will always have all you need for yourselves
and more than enough for every good cause."
— 2 Corinthians 9:8 (GNT)

God's intention is not for you to live in poverty. How do I know this? Because He did not give you the "power to be poor" (Deuteronomy 8:18). Therefore, if God has given you the "power to get wealth" and you do not get it, who's to blame?

To put it plainly, "poverty is a choice".

Ok, ok, I can already hear the naysayers, "but what about all the people who can't control their circumstances because they were born into impoverished conditions?"

The truth is, there will always be people who are less fortunate, but that does not mean you have to be (or stay) one of them.

What did Jesus mean when He said, *"the poor you will have with you always"* *(John 12:8)?*

"Poverty" is a mindset that creates a consequence of thought that people find themselves in without understanding they have paralyzed themselves by thinking they are helpless in (what they deem) a hopeless situation. They feel things will never get better and remain stuck there, often through self-sabotaging behaviors, thus becoming a self-fulfilling prophecy.

Yes, folks can be born into impoverished conditions, but most people justify their choice to remain poor because they feel they are victims of their circumstances or their environment. This is why poverty will always exist (John 12:8), because there will continually be people who make excuses not to put forth the effort or action necessary to change their situation by using what God gave them. The ability to accomplish and achieve whatever we aspire to (Genesis 11:6). He has given us ALL a measure of faith (Romans 12:3) and with faith the size of a mustard seed, we can move mountains (Matthew 17:20). Jesus said, *"If thou canst believe, all things are possible to him that believeth"* *(Mark 9:23).*

In the same way that getting wealth requires a certain process, being/staying poor necessitates a certain way of thinking.

LABOR *NOT* TO BE RICH

The Bible says in Proverbs 23:4, "labor not to be rich…"

In other words, God gave you the power to have more than enough. (2 Corinthians 9:8)

Why?

You are "blessed to be a blessing" (Genesis 12:2). In every instance where you see God releasing blessings upon his people, it is always an overflow (or in abundance), which brings us back to rich versus wealth.

When you hear the word "rich," how does it make you feel?

For many people, there is a "notion of negativity" associated with the word. Ever heard the statement "too rich for my blood?"

When they hear a person is rich, some may assume that person is probably selfish, greedy, and just wasting their money buying unnecessary and frivolous stuff. They believe rich people only care about themselves, while living in their big houses, driving their fancy cars, and scoffing at the little person trying to make it.

Ironically, these same people who think rich people "are the worst," feel they would *"do good"* if they had those riches.

Therefore, they have negative thoughts and feelings about a thing they secretly wish/want to be.

However, think about the word "wealth" for a moment. It does not conjure negative connotations like the word "rich."

Think about which sounds better, to be a part of a "get rich quick scheme" or to "learn the ways of wealth"?

WHAT IS WEALTH?

If *Rich* means "having too much" and *Wealth* means "having more than enough," what is the difference?

Simply put, "rich" is excess to the point of waste, whereas "wealth" is abundance to the point of blessing.

This is why God said, *"labor not to be rich" (Proverbs 23:4)*, because He gave you *"the power to get wealth" (Deuteronomy 8:18)*.

Wealth is a Godly overflow for the purpose of being a blessing to the people around you and the world in general.

In what way are you able to be a blessing? By using what God gave you!

God gave you a gift, an assignment, something that He wants to accomplish *with and through* YOU.

It's through this gift that you will walk out your purpose and fulfill your destiny. This is how you will be all God has created you to be, do all God has created you to do, and have all God has created you to have.

It is through this gift that you will be a blessing on the earth. (I will deal with this in greater detail in chapters 2 and 5.)

"MONEY" MENTALITY

When you talk about money (especially as a preacher), people begin to feel all sorts of ways. Because of this, I have come to the conclusion that there are three types of *"Gospels"* regarding money;

- **The Prosperity Gospel**

Money matters the most; this is the "be *Rich* angle."

This is the gospel where some slick-talking reverend/preacher is telling you, "God is in the *blessing business*, sow a seed and He will meet your need, name it and claim it" (i.e., *blab it and grab it*). You should just sit back and wait on God, but say it in a way that removes any responsibility on your part. It is the preaching that suggests God only wants to bless you and that's it, as though you have some sort of God given entitlement. Therefore, we treat God as though He is a "genie in a bottle" that is at our beck and call to grant our every wish.

I want to be clear; there is nothing wrong with "speaking it into existence" (Romans 4:17) or by faith sowing seeds and believing God for a harvest (the Bible is full of stories of how God was able to take little and make much or use small portions for BIG purposes.

What I am talking about here is manipulation, those false prophets who will take advantage of your *needs* to fulfill "their own" *wants*.

- **The Poverty Gospel**

Money is a messy matter; this is the "be *Poor* approach."

They come against the *prosperity gospel*. These are the preachers who say you should never focus on money. They try to connect it to this idea that money should never matter. You should be happy with little, always trying to live on less. This is seen as a noble virtue or as though being poor has an element of piety attached to it. Why? You ask…, they will argue because "Jesus was poor," He had nowhere to lay his head (Luke 9:58) or how can a rich man make it into heaven, it is harder than a camel going through the eye of a needle (Matthew 19:24). These preachers say, "money is the root to all evil" (notice what's missing, because they always leave out one important word, 1 Timothy 6:10).

Again, let me be clear: modesty and moderation have their place, especially in the form of Godly and wise stewardship (1 Corinthians 4:2).

But this is not what they preach; they will say lavish living is of the devil, and a desire for more than the minimum is ungodly.

Regarding either of these "wrong schools of thought," no matter the angle or approach, they each have an agenda that is not based on truth!

*The real issue here is that they both require you to take and twist scripture out of context.**

- **The Practical Gospel**

Money is not "ALL" that matters; this is the "be *Wealthy* attitude."

This means you keep money in its proper perspective. It is a tool that God gives you to use. You use it to glorify and upbuild the kingdom of God through your gifts and your actions (Matt 5:16), and in so doing, God does not mind if you are blessed in the process.

When you see a scripture like "Money answers all things" (Eccl. 10:19), it is not claiming that money is the *be-all, end-all,* but rather it is highlighting wisdom vs. foolishness. Because money makes you more of what you already are; if you are a wise person, you will be wise with money, but if you are a foolish person, you will be foolish with money (Luke 16:10).

Therefore, our focus should not be on just having more money (in and of itself, although we do need it); our focus should be on how we become better so we can "do more, with more".

There is something to be said for not settling for less; you should have the mindset to always go for more.

However, for most of us, when it comes to money, the problem is our mindset. The quality of your thoughts regarding money will dictate the quantity of money you can receive. How you think about money determines how much money can or cannot be released to you. Although most of us would hate to admit it, the truth is—we *are not ready for a lot of the things we pray for* (James 4:3). And God is not in the business of *wasting*; He will not give you something you are not ready for.

> *"God is faithful; he will not let you be tempted*
> *beyond what you can bear."*
> **— 1 Corinthians 10:13 (NIV)**

When most people hear this scripture, they typically think it only applies to them when they are going through something negative. Therefore, they read 1 Corinthians 10:13 with the filter that everyone goes through things and is tempted, but God will always make a way out. Naturally, we believe that if a "way of escape" must be made, then it has to be from something bad because there is no need to escape from anything good, right?

Unless, by giving you what is good before you can handle it, then it becomes bad because of what you are tempted to do with it.

ARE YOU "REALLY" READY?

Consider the story of the Prodigal Son (Luke 15:11-32). Here is an individual who got exactly what he wanted when he wanted it. *"Give me the portion of goods that falleth to me" (Luke 15:12),* he told his father. And in an instant, he became rich.

The problem, as the story goes, was that he was clearly not ready to be blessed like that, even though he got exactly what he asked for.

The Bible says that he *"wasted his substance with riotous living and when he had spent all, there arose a mighty famine in that land; and he began to be in want"* (Luke 15:13-14). Because he got what he could not handle, he wasted it. When a famine came, he was not prepared and fell on hard times. This is when God made a way of escape. The Bible says, *"he came to himself"* (Luke 15:17), which means he tapped into the power within himself—he tapped into the power of God.

> *"Ye are of God, because greater is HE (meaning God) that is in you,*
> *than he (meaning you) that is in the world."*
> **— 1 John 4:4**
> *(Emphasis in parentheses is my own)*

When we *"come to ourselves,"* we can think with a level of clarity that shows how much we have *grown* through the process and how God is making a way out. From that place of clarity, we can commit to a plan of action that will change our situation. This proves that if you are not in a place now that you want to be in, then you can change it. Tap into the inner strength at the core of your being. Realize that you are better than this, and your present situation will not be your permanent situation. You don't have to stay here!

Take a stand—commit that you will do what it takes to change it.

I dare you to "COME TO YOURSELF!"

This is why mindset is so critical. We show our maturity by our mentality, and the more you "grow" as a person, the further you can "go" as a person. Maturity is directly tied to wisdom—it is not enough to just know what to do, but you must do what you know. The Bible states that after the prodigal son *"came to himself,"* he said, *"I will arise..."* (verse 18), then *"he arose..."* (verse 20).

> *"Even so faith, if it hath not works, is dead, being alone."*
> **— James 2:17**

Just as the Prodigal Son understood, nothing would change in his life unless he "got up" and did something about it. He said what he was going to do, and then he did it!

Your thoughts **must** become actions. This is the only thing that leads to accomplishment.

It is time for you to ARISE!

> *"Arise,*
> *shine; for thy light is come,*
> *and the glory of the Lord is risen upon thee."*
> **— Isaiah 60:1**

There is a shift that is getting ready to happen in your life!

It is a Shift from Struggle to Significance, Strength, and Success!!!

MPOWER ME

CHAPTER 1

Shift—Be, Do, Have

"You must stop being the old you, so you can start being the new you."
— **Anonymous**

WHAT IS A PARADIGM?

Most people are familiar with the term "Paradigm Shift" without a full working knowledge of where the term comes from. Well, it has its origins in science, from a philosopher named Thomas Kuhn. He coined this term as a means to describe an accepted way of thinking (in the scientific community) that has now *shifted* as a result of new evidence. It ultimately spread from there and eventually, "Paradigm Shift" came to mean anything (in life) that was "game-changing."

But, to understand what it means to have a Paradigm shift (scientifically), you first must have a notion of what Thomas Kuhn would say a paradigm is;

> *A paradigm… is a general theory that helps to provide scientists working in a particular field with their broad theoretical framework… It provides them with their basic assumptions, their key concepts, and their methodology. It gives general direction and goals for their research.* [3]

---

[3] Westacott, Emrys. "What Is a Paradigm Shift?" ThoughtCo, January 22, 2019, www.thoughtco.com/what-is-a-paradigm-shift-2670671

Let me explain how this applies to you. I'm sure you have heard the term *"thinking outside the box."* This is said to encourage someone to go beyond their normal mode of thinking. Well, the *"box"* mentioned here is the paradigm.

I am choosing to start our journey here, so you have a full understanding that your present paradigm is "why" you are, "where" you are.

From the definition above, we can see that a *Paradigm* is the standard or set of rules that control one's viewpoint. You have a collection of concepts that become beliefs known as a *paradigm*; this is the foundational framework from which you operate every day. It is your subconscious conditioning that comes from a multitude of habits.

My definition of a paradigm is the "practiced personal programming of a person or people." This programming is created by the belief and behavior that have been modeled repeatedly for you. Once you begin to personalize it and put it into practice, it becomes your paradigm.

Paradigms are created early in life by external influences (such as what other people tell you), and later in life by internal influences (i.e., what you tell yourself).

It is extremely important that you know this before we move on because it will determine what happens from this point forward.

REJECT OR PERFECT

"I call heaven and earth to record this day against you, that I have set before you life and death, blessing and cursing: therefore choose life, that both thou and thy seed may live"
— **Deuteronomy 30:1**

In the Bible, we find a very common story called the "parable of the sower." Jesus said, "The sower went forth to sow" (Matthew 13:3-9); He then proceeded to talk about how the seed (that was sown) fell on four different types of ground...

What I get from this passage is that there are really only four things you can do with any idea that is introduced/presented to you.

You can either:

- Reject it (seed fell by the wayside),
- Neglect it (seed fell on stony ground),
- Select, but not Protect it (seed fell among thorns),

OR

- Accept and Perfect it (seed fell on good ground).

The question then becomes, how will you treat the idea of what God is trying to sow into your life right now?

BE, DO, HAVE

Now that you know what a paradigm is, are you ready to shift?

I will answer for you... It is a resounding YES!

You have been stuck where you are long enough!!!

A paradigm shift is a radical change in underlying beliefs or theory. You can shift your paradigm by taking a quantum leap of faith, so you can advance into a new realm of unlimited possibility that says you can exercise the power God gave you.

To shift your paradigm, you must be willing (by faith) to completely abandon your old mindset and embrace the mentality that says first you must BE the best version of yourself, then DO the actions necessary to HAVE what it is you want. You begin this new paradigm by becoming your best self now, then developing the "Discipline of Doing," which will lead you to having the life you want to have.

"BE, DO, HAVE"—these are the three levels of Paradigms that you need to shift.

This ideal of "Be, Do, Have" is an important fundamental concept for you to accept.

It is a foundational *process* in achieving success.

I italicized the word "process" because many attempt to accomplish things in the wrong order. Most people want to start at the "Having" level, but this is not where real change occurs. Then they may go to the "**DO**ing" level, but this is only temporary. If you don't begin from the "**BE**ing" level, then you can never become that which you desire.

> "And God said unto Moses, **I Am That I Am.**"
> — **Exodus 3:14**

The above Scripture is God's response to Moses when he asked Him, "Who shall I say sent me?" (Exodus 3:13).

The reason I pointed it out is because I want to focus on the statement, "*I am that I am.*"

Be — I am

Do — that

Have — I AM

20

The BE, DO, HAVE way of life is very important for you to grasp because it is "I am that I am!" Look at how God is telling Moses what is about to happen.

It is a pattern for us to go from *"where we are* to where *we want to be."*

Bob Proctor, considered one of the world's foremost authorities on success, once said, "To be truly successful, you must give yourself a target to shoot for (through Be, Do, Have)," by answering these three questions:

1. Who do you want to be?
2. What do you want to do?
3. What do you want to have?

Why is it important to ask these questions in this particular order? Because, you have what you are. I know you glossed over that last sentence, but stop and let that sink in for a moment—again, I will repeat it:

YOU HAVE WHAT YOU ARE!

Therefore, if you want to have more, **BE** more!!

Be the change you want to see, be the difference you want to make. It begins with YOU!

At some point, you have to let go of who you used to be and come to grips with who you can be.

> *"Therefore, if any man be in Christ,*
> *he is a new creature: old things are passed away;*
> *behold, all things are become new."*
> **— 2 Corinthians 5:17**

BE — The present embodiment today of that which you desire tomorrow.

You don't *become* who you want to *be; you* must *be* who you want to *become.*

This is your Identity; it requires clarity and conviction.

DO — Actions that align with who you are now BE*ing* in your journey to becoming.

This is your Implementation; it requires commitment and consistency.

HAVE — Embracing the reality of your manifested desires... This is when God says, "Go in and possess the land." (Deuteronomy 3:18)

This is your Integration; it requires courage and confidence.

So, what does this look like in reality?

Really, there are only two ways to shift your paradigm: either through Emotional Implantation or Repetition. The first way is outside of your control, and the second way is within your control.

EMOTIONAL IMPLANTATION

Emotional implantation is a turning point that happens when an occurrence or event impacts you so drastically that it instantly changes who you are. Examples include an unexpected windfall or significant blessing, surviving a near-death experience, miraculously healing from a critical disease, but also being told you have a critical disease, suffering the loss of a very close loved one, or some other type of painful news or incident.

Something like this has the potential to immediately shift your paradigm. This can happen from something, either so terrifically good, or something that is perceived as horrifically bad. If it is sensational or traumatic enough, it can shock your system into a whole new way of believing and behaving. It has been proven that a person's whole attitude and approach to life and what is truly important can shift in a flash because of an experience like this.

Maybe you know what I am talking about?

Have you ever been through something that was exceptionally painful or extraordinarily pleasant and that you were never the same after that? Well, that was a paradigm shift via an emotional implant that changed you from that point on.

Typically, an *"Emotional Implantation"* is not within your control, but this next way of shifting your Paradigm is.

REPETITION

"Repetition" is the number one way of reprogramming your subconscious mind.

But it has to be repeated information that you are emotionally transfixed by, something that you deeply feel and that you constantly visualize and verbalize.

As I previously said, *Paradigms* are created early in life by external influences (such as what other people tell you) and later in life by internal influences (i.e., what you tell yourself).

This happens through "Repetition."

When you experience anything (be it good or bad) repeatedly, this routine of repetition creates new neural pathways in your subconscious mind.

This, in turn, is reflected in how you formulate your own framework and function.

Remember when I said, "Revelation is Reinforced through Repetition?"

It is the power of affirmations, which is based on Romans 10:17, which states, *Faith cometh by hearing.*

Anything that you hear constantly increases belief in the thing being heard.

This is true from both a negative and a positive perspective.

Any negative messaging that is reinforced verbally (either by you or someone of influence in your life) will cause you to believe you only get undesirable outcomes by embedding in your subconscious mind that things will not work out for you and that you are not good enough.

That is how negative paradigms are created.

To create a new paradigm, you need to do the opposite.

Therefore, Romans 10:17 goes on to say, *"and hearing by the Word of God."*

All positive messaging reinforced verbally (either by you or someone of influence in your life) will build your faith to believe in a positive outcome.

This is why BE, DO, and HAVE are so critical. Here, you begin the process of manifestation by decreeing and declaring, "I AM that I am!"

In the beginning, you may be "…calling those things that be not as though they were" (Romans 4:17), but the more you *SAY it*, the more you *SEE it*, and that belief turns into behavior.

As you continue to "talk the talk" and "walk the walk," a metamorphosis takes place.

Because the positive repetition in God's Word is embedded in your subconscious mind, that things will work out for you.

Romans 8:28 tells us,
*"And we know that all things work together for good to them that love God,
to them who are the called according to His purpose."*

From that perspective, it is clear to see how God himself desires to reinforce this positivity in your life no matter what.

Our job is to believe and walk in that truth so that no matter what we are going through, we know we are going to the place that God has predestined for us.

You can change your Paradigm by repeatedly reinforcing this notion: "It will work in MY favor."

This is the truth of God's Word and God's promise to you.

TIME FOR A BREAKTHROUGH

To shift your situation, you must see that the solution lies in accepting responsibility for your role in its creation.

Only then can you change.

I am not talking about changing just for the sake of changing. I am talking about intentionally becoming the person you know you can be.

We will talk much more in-depth about how to get your breakthrough throughout this book. But for now, just know the *best* version of you begins with being a *better* you now

It is time for a breakthrough, and it begins now.

Tony Robbins gives "3 *Steps to a Breakthrough*"[4] that I really like:

- ❖ *Change your Strategy.*
- ❖ *Change your Story.*
- ❖ *Change your State.*

---

[4] Robbins, Tony. The 3 Steps to a Breakthrough. 2015, https://www.tonyrobbins.com/podcasts/3-steps-breakthrough/

CHANGE YOUR STRATEGY

Albert Einstein is widely credited for once saying, "The definition of insanity is doing the same thing over and over again but expecting different results." He was also the one who said, "We cannot solve our problems with the same level of thinking we used when we created them." We will dive deeper into that quote later in this book, but for now, the point is understanding that the first step to get a breakthrough (according to Tony Robbins) is "Changing your Strategy."

Logically, that seems to make a lot of sense: if what you are doing is not working, then do something different. Amazingly, though, we often get stuck in the "this-is-the-way-we-do-things-around-here" thinking that does not yield the results we are looking for. Change your strategy!

Take a new look at your situation, be solution-oriented and not problem-focused. Ask yourself this question: What is it that I can do differently to solve this issue? When the answer comes, take action. If it does not work, then ask the question again with an emphasis on the word "differently." Then do something different, but keep going, until you succeed and get your breakthrough.

To change your Situation, change your Strategy.

CHANGE YOUR STORY

What the devil desires is for us to remember our story in a way that hurts us and does not help us. A great example of this is in Genesis 3. Here, we read about the interaction between Eve and the devil, who are having a conversation about God's instructions in the Garden of Eden. The devil asked Eve a question, "hath God said…" and from there Eve's mind took over and changed things so that as she remembered it, she told herself a different story than what God actually said (Genesis 2:16-17, 3:1-6).

What story are you telling yourself that is keeping you from your breakthrough? It is not always some devil who gets us to remember a twisted version of the truth. Sometimes, we are the ones who cause our own harm because when we narrate the plot, the part we often play is that of the victim instead of the victor.

Sometimes our worst attacks don't come from anything external.

Sometimes it is the internal story we keep telling ourselves that hurts us the most.

Our worst "enemy" is the "inner me."

Your story is the unique set of circumstances that make up who you are. It is the collection of experiences you have had, and when you look back on them, you realize they had a profound effect on you and the person you have become.

Your story can create a paradigm, be it positive or negative.

Does it only bring you pain when you rehash the set of events? Does it still make you cry from the hurt when you think about it? Here is a powerful question: Why? What is "your" version of the way it happened? What are your thoughts and feelings about the way it affected you?

What is your narrative?

The way you narrate your life story (to yourself and others) and the impact certain things had on you will cause you to either stay stuck or move forward. Most people think that the story has the power, but the truth of the matter is that the power lies in "HOW" you tell the story.

That is why the Bible says that we are overcome by the "words" of our testimony (Revelation 12:11).

When you tell your story, are you looking for sympathy? Are you looking for someone to feel sorry for you? Or in telling your story, you find it gives you strength and power, and you are able to look back at the fact that you were able to not only survive through it, but *thrive* through it?

What is your narrative?

You may not have had control over what you went through, but when you look back and tell the story, you have complete control over how you frame it.

No matter how bad it was, tell the good. No matter how negative it was, tell the positive. No matter how dark the days are, tell me about the light at the end of the tunnel. No matter how long you were in it, tell how God brought you out, how He made a way, how it strengthened you during the process, how you came out better and not bitter as a result of what you went through!

To change your Situation, change your Story.

CHANGE YOUR STATE

Your "state of mind" is by far the most critical component to you receiving your breakthrough.

Of the greatest gifts that God has given to us, the human mind is the single most powerful force on the planet outside of the human spirit.

If you want to change your situation, then change your mind.

We will dive very deep into the subject of "Mentality/Mindset" in Chapter 6, but for now, let's focus on your state, which Tony Robbins says is the most important one to change.

In the book, The Developing Mind, author Daniel J. Siegel describes a 'state of mind' in this way:

One can discover the elements of an individual's State of Mind by focusing on the elements of his/her perceptions, feelings, thoughts, memories, attitudes, beliefs, and desires and how these may be influencing his/her behavior and interactions with others.

States can become traits of the individual that influence both internal and interpersonal processes. The regulation of emotion directs the flow of energy through the changing states of activation of the brain. A state of mind can be proposed to be a pattern of activation of recruited systems within the brain responsible for (1) perceptual bias, (2) emotional tone and regulation, (3) memory processes, (4) mental models, and (5) behavioral response patterns.[5]

This is the scientific way of stating a spiritual truth, which is—your state of mind has a direct impact and effect on your life and reality. Biblically put, Proverbs 23:7 tells us, *for as a man thinketh in his heart, so is he.*

As Napoleon Hill says in his blockbuster book, Think and Grow Rich, "Thoughts are things and powerful things at that."[6]

Your breakthrough is dependent upon your understanding that your state of mind dictates your results.

To change your Situation, change your State.

EQUIPPED TO SUCCEED

You have been thoroughly and fully equipped to succeed. The truth of the matter is, you have more at your disposal than you may ever know or even believe. God, in His infinite wisdom, gave you everything you would ever need to accomplish all that He has ordained for you to do.

---

[5] Siegel, Daniel J. The Developing Mind (New York: The Guilford Press; 2012); pages 210-211

[6] Hill, Napoleon. Think and Grow Rich (New York: Skyhorse; 2016); page 19

"According as His divine power hath given unto us all things that pertain unto life and godliness, through the knowledge of Him that hath called us to glory and virtue."
— 2 Peter 1:3

But you must utilize your faith to take advantage of the gift of God within you. How do you move forward with what God has shown you, even though you feel things keep getting in your way, including yourself (doubts, inhibitions, anxieties, fears, questions, etc.)? You may not feel ready, but you know it is "now-or-never" to see all your dreams come true.

What do you do then?

MOVE MADE

"Don't be upset by the results you didn't get; from the work you did not do."
— Eric Thomas
"The Hip Hop Preacher"

I want to share a story with you that will answer that question.

One morning, while I was driving into work, I was listening to the radio, and little did I know that I would hear a phrase that would drastically change my life. Canton Jones, a Pastor and Gospel Artist, was a guest deejay covering for Pastor and Gospel Artist Erica Campbell on her radio show, "Get Up Mornings with Erica Campbell." Erica Campbell has a segment on her show where she shares some encouraging and edifying words called "The Faith Walk."

For his "Faith Walk," Canton Jones read from the Scripture in James 2, which states, "faith without works is dead." He went on to say that he wanted to focus on people who have dreams that they keep putting off.

He said, "I want to tell you that FAITH equals a move made!"

The strength of the statement was in its simplicity. It shot through me like a bullet.

FAITH EQUALS A MOVE MADE!

He went on to reference the Biblical story of the woman with the issue of blood, found in Mark 5:25-34. If you are not familiar with the story, it is about a woman who was sick for twelve years, and nothing she did up to that point worked or healed her. She exhausted herself and her resources, and the Bible says, *"She was no better, but rather grew worse."* Mark 5:26.

Have you ever been in a situation where everything you tried to do *in your own power* to fix the situation failed miserably? Well, this was the plight of this woman. Then one day she heard that Jesus was passing by, and after having *"spent all… she said within herself; if I can but touch the hem of His garment, I shall be made whole."* Mark 5:27-28. She risked everything to make her move. Canton Jones ultimately said she would have missed her breakthrough if she had not acted in that moment.

He followed up with, *"YOU GOT TO MAKE YOUR MOVE!!"*

I tell you that story because on the day I heard it, I knew God Himself was speaking directly to me! I could not keep letting days pass by without making the moves I needed to make to change my current situation. I knew then that this season in time was my window of opportunity. I had already let too much of the window close with procrastination, laziness, excuses, and self-pity. For far too long, I had let my dream of success lie dormant and become stagnant.

At that moment, God said, *"Roger, there is so much you are not doing, yet you are expecting results!"*

For me, it was now or never. God said MAKE A MOVE!!

I made up my mind then that I would not just sit around wishing things would get better or feeling sorry for myself with a "woe-is-me" attitude.

31

I knew only action would lead to accomplishment!

What about you? Are you ready to make your move?

Or will you keep hoping and wishing the things going on in your life will get better by themselves?

Here is a truth I learned: you must be present to win!

Will you continue to allow time to just go on without getting involved in fixing your life?

Know this: it won't change unless you change it.

Like I said earlier, you know what to do; you simply are not doing what you know!

Faith equals a move made.

I dare you to make your move!!

MPOWER ME

CHAPTER 2

"Then"...
You Shall Have Good Success

Success does not require that you look out the window;
Success only requires that you look in the mirror.
— **Eric Thomas**
"The Hip Hop Preacher"

THE DEFINITION OF SUCCESS

Not everyone sees success the same way.

It can mean completely different things to different people.

❖ Legendary Basketball Coach John Wooden said, "Success is peace of mind, which is a direct result of self-satisfaction in knowing you did your best to become the best you are capable of becoming."

❖ Sir Winston Churchill said, "Success is going from failure to failure and not losing enthusiasm."

❖ Napoleon Hill (who wrote the "bible of business," *Think and Grow Rich*) said, "SUCCESS is the attainment of your DEFINITE CHIEF AIM without violating the rights of other people."

❖ Earl Nightingale (considered the Dean of Personal Development) said, "Success is really nothing more than the progressive realization of a worthy ideal. This means that any person who knows what they are doing and where they are going is a success. Any person with a goal towards which they are working is a successful person."

The official definition in the Merriam-Webster Dictionary defines success as: *the fact of getting or achieving wealth, respect, or fame; the correct or desired result of an attempt; someone or something that is successful; a person or thing that succeeds.*

My definition of success is:

The Achievement of any God-given Aim, for which you have been both Assigned and Anointed.

So here is a question for you: how do you define success?

Here is a better question: How does God define success?

> *"This book of the law shall not depart out of thy mouth; but thou shalt meditate therein day and night, that thou mayest observe to do according to all that is written therein: for then thou shalt make thy way prosperous, and then thou shalt have **good success.**"*
> **— Joshua 1:8 (Emphasis added)**

When we look at how God uses the word success here, it is preceded by the word "good."

I find that interesting because we can infer that if there is a "good" success, then there must also be a "bad" success.

We do not have to look far to figure out what bad success is, either. We can see that God gives Joshua some very specific instructions to put himself in a position to succeed. If Joshua follows these instructions, God says, "THEN you will have good success." This clearly means that God's divine will is for a person to be successful. Therefore, bad success is anything achieved in a way that is outside of God's will. (We will talk more about that later; for now, I just wanted to point it out.)

So, God defines success as *the Speaking, Thinking, and Doing of His Word.*

THE SECRET TO SUCCESS

The Secret to Success is that there really is no "secret to success"!

I understand you may have seen movies on the subject (e.g., "The Secret"), or heard about "sweatless victories." Certainly, you have read about God miraculously blessing people financially, but even with that being said, there is no "magic wand for wealth."

That may come as a shock to some and not as a surprise to others. The truth of the matter is you can't get away from the worth of working for it.

However, the *"work"* I am referring to here is not aimlessly beating your head against the wall to make it work at all costs. That is not the secret.

It will be working with the Will of God, then "It Will Work, if You Work it."

But let's say, for the sake of argument, there was a secret to success. The wonderful thing about God is that He would not hide it from you; it would be in plain sight—in His Word.

> *"This book of the law shall not depart out of thy mouth; but thou shalt meditate therein day and night, that thou mayest observe to do according to all that is written therein: for **then** thou shalt make thy way prosperous, and **then** thou shalt have good success."*
> — Joshua 1:8

*"Blessed is the man that walketh not in the counsel of the ungodly, nor standeth in the way of sinners, nor sitteth in the seat of the scornful. But his delight is in the Law of the Lord; and in His Law doth he meditate day and night. **And** he shall be like a tree planted by the rivers of water, that bringeth forth his fruit in his season; his leaf also shall not wither; and whatsoever he doeth shall prosper."*
— Psalm 1:1-3

*"Beloved, I wish above all things that thou mayest prosper and be in health, **even as** thy soul prospereth."*
— 3 John 1:2

If we look at these scriptures, we notice a pattern. In each one, we find what I call a *"conditional clause."*

What is a conditional clause, you ask?

In each scripture mentioned, there are certain things that God is saying you can have, but these things are contingent upon your actions.

That means: You can have the Promise if you meet the Prerequisite.

In each passage, the conditional clauses are as follows:

- ❖ Joshua 1: 8... "then"...
- ❖ Psalms 1:1-3... "And"...
- ❖ John 1:2... "even as"...

These clauses either come before or after the condition(s), depending on the scripture.

So, if you see it there in plain sight, how then is it a secret?

Because the secret is in the steps one must take to achieve it.

Businessman Albert Gray once did a study on successful people and found they all possessed one characteristic above all else.

In a keynote address entitled, "The New Common Denominator of Success," which he delivered in 1940, Gray stated, "The common denominator of success—the secret of success of every person who has ever been successful—lies in the fact that he or she formed the habit of doing things that failures don't like to do."

To put it another way;

"Successful people do what unsuccessful people are unwilling to do."

If there were a secret, it would be this: the answer is not in *"wishing"* for it, but in *"Working"* for it. And truthfully, almost everyone wishes for success, but not everyone is willing to do the work. "Wishing" is the equivalent of waiting on the elevator to get to the next level and wondering why it is taking so long.

While "working" is the equivalent of taking the stairs.

Side note: If you happen to be one of those people waiting on that elevator, I am sorry to inform you that the elevator to success has been, and always will be, broken. The escalator is also down and in need of repair, in case you wondered.

There are no shortcuts!

THE WAY TO WEALTH

> *"A good man leaves an inheritance to his children's children:*
> *and the **wealth** of the sinner is **laid up** for the just."*
> **—Proverbs 13:22**
> *(Some translations use the word "wicked" instead of "sinner.")*

I have an interesting take on this scripture.

Like I said in the disclaimer, even if you disagree, at least listen to my point, and hopefully I can persuade you to see what I am saying.

Now, this is not a hermeneutical exegesis, so I am asking all you theologians for some latitude.

Typically, when this scripture is read, the most popular interpretation is that the "wealth of the sinners" referenced here is talking about all the rich people in the earth who don't know God.

"The just" are all the Christians who know God and are waiting on this "BIG wealth transfer" that is "laid up."

Allow me to offer another point of view:

1. The scripture begins by telling us God's definition of a "good man."

    It is a person who leaves enough real money (not only wisdom, but literal inheritance) to last at least two generations (and beyond).

2. After this, it says the wealth of the sinner/wicked is laid up for the just.

    In its simplest definition, the word "sinner/wicked" here means a person who is outside of the will of God. Transversely, the word "just" here means a person who is in the will of God. Why is that an important distinction to make?

Because the typical assertion is that these are two different people.

But is it outside of the realm of possibility for this to be the same person?

My answer is "No," and here is why I believe that.

I will use myself as an example, going back to when I had a "regular job." There isn't anything wrong with a regular job, but I'm talking about when I was working at a job just to pay the bills. Not work that I was particularly interested in; just doing what I had to do to take care of my family.

I was hardly on my way to wealth.

I was living paycheck to paycheck, "robbing Peter to pay Paul"—on the proverbial grind, if you know what I mean.

There was a longing in me that knew I was created for something far greater, but meanwhile, I knew I was outside of God's will for my life.

"If my people, which are called by my name, shall humble themselves, and pray, and seek my face, and turn from their 'wicked ways'; then will I hear from heaven, and will forgive their sin, and will heal their land."
— 2 Chronicles 7:14 (Emphasis added)

In the above scripture, we can clearly see that God is letting the people know that for Him to move on their behalf, there is a change they first need to make.

If you combine Proverbs 13:22 with 2 Chronicles 7:14, we discover the wealth of the sinner/wicked (those outside of God's will) is laid up for the just (those in God's will). So, how do they go from sinner to just?

Here we see a Four-Step Process:

1. Humble themselves (1 Peter 5:6)
2. Pray (Luke 18:1)
3. Seek God's Face (Psalms 27:8)
4. Turn from their "wicked" ways (Psalms 37:27-29)

It is clear to see the connection: the wealth was laid up as long as they were outside of God's will. God told them how to correct it and **then** (conditional clause) He released what was laid up (i.e., He healed their land).

Have you ever felt like there has to be more? Like you should be doing more, and was created for more? When you close your eyes, do you picture a different life for yourself? A life of joy, peace, fulfillment, inspiration, and purpose? A life of impact, where you are pursuing your passion and making a difference? Does that life you picture seem as real as your current reality, as though you are looking at who you could be, seeing your potential realized?

Well, let me assure you that what you picture is possible.

This is God's will for your life. What you picture is what is laid up for you.

So, how do you get it?

BE the person you see (this is the way to wealth).

The only difference between who you are and who you were meant to be is that you have to get in *right standing* with God.

Remember in the introduction when I proved Biblically that God will only release to the righteous?

All you must do is get in the will of God for your life.

Transition from the person who does just enough to scrape by, to BE*ing* the person who does what you are purposed to do.

It is a process, yes.

I am not saying to foolishly quit your job and blindly chase some dream life.

What I am saying though, is that the wealth mentioned in Proverbs 13:22 is not someone else's, it is yours.

And in this book, I will give you what is necessary to "unlock" all that is *laid up* for you.

But before there can be manifestation, there must first be transformation.

> *"It is pleasant to see dreams come true,*
> *but fools refuse to turn from evil to attain them."*
> **— Proverbs 13:19 (NLT)**

THE LOCK

Proverbs 13:22 mentions wealth that is "laid up" (which, I am translating this "wealth" as SUCCESS: meaning if you are successful, then you can leave this inheritance to your children's children.)

I want to give you a scenario regarding the phrase "laid up."

Picture in your mind a common three-number dial style combination master lock, maybe like the one you had in grade school for your locker. Imagine I hand you this lock and tell you to open it. You look back at me, waiting for me to say the next obvious thing, but I say nothing, other than to reiterate my previous instruction. So, you ask the obvious question, "What is the combination?"

Now that we have established that there is some critical information you must know before you can open this lock, I proceed to tell you a bunch of random numbers, and then I tell you to open the lock. You give me a confused look and say, "That is too many numbers. You know this style lock only takes three numbers, and those numbers must be in a certain order."

I give you the three numbers in the proper sequence, but then I ask you to please hand me the lock back, and tell you to open the lock without touching it. You can't do anything to physically grab the lock to open it. You can think about opening it, to see if the power of your mind will work. Or you can try speaking to it, naming it, and claiming it. But none of that works; it still won't open.

Finally, I give you the lock so that you can open it. Now, you know the correct combination. So, you turn right three times, stopping at the first digit. Turn left one full turn, passing the first number, and stop at the second digit. Turn right and stop at the third digit. You pull the shackle, and VOILA!

The lock opens.

Does the lock care who you are?

Does it care about how young or old you are, or if you are male or female? Does it care about your weight/shape, your looks, or your education? Does it care about your race or ethnicity? How about where you are from, where you were born, who your family is, the environment in which you were raised, or your upbringing? Does it care if you are handicapped, or have a disability, or were diagnosed with whatever?

It doesn't matter what you think is negative about you; the question is, does the lock care?

The answers to all these questions are a unanimous **NO**!

The lock is oblivious to the "Who"—it will open for anyone who knows and inputs the correct combination.

So, how does this common combination lock relate to our discussion about what is "laid up" for you?

The answer is threefold.

ACCEPTANCE

The first thing I did in our scenario earlier was hand you a lock and told you to open it. You automatically knew this type of lock required a combination to be opened. It is easy to see that it's impossible to open the lock without the combination (hence the name). To do so, you must first "know something." This knowledge is crucial if you are going to get the lock opened. What I'm referring to here must be accepted as truth. It doesn't matter whether you believe it or not. Even if you resist it, that won't change the facts. There is no way around it; you must accept that it is impossible for me to open this lock, if I don't have the combination.

Here is another way to put it: there is a law governing this lock. This law requires that I know the combination, or else I can't open it. I may even watch other people open the lock, but until I know the combination, I cannot get it unlocked. It has nothing to do with all the things we call setbacks and disadvantages (mentioned earlier) as to why the lock won't open. Or if life has dealt me a bad hand. If I know the combination, the lock will open. If I don't, the lock will not open. This must be accepted as a fact. Just like there is a law that governs lock, there are also laws that govern success.

I submit unto you that knowing how to operate within and take advantage of those laws is what will unlock success in your life. Can you imagine all the people in the world trying to unlock this lock without the combination? How frustrating could that be?

ACCURACY

Going back to the lock scenario, when you asked for the combination, I gave you a bunch of random numbers. Well, it didn't work, and I'll tell you why. It is the equivalent of me giving you what you need to know, then mixing in there a bunch of unhelpful information. It is like trying to find a needle in a haystack.

In your quest for success, it can be very easy to be inundated with an overwhelming amount of information on the subject. Some of it is extremely useful and effective, and some is not so much. The problem is that it is all mixed up together. Do a Google search on the word *success,* and you will find page after page of information, instruction, and just plain old opinion, with all of them saying their way to achieve success is the right way. But the true question in all this is, what is the best way for you?

Because knowing a bunch of unhelpful stuff is useless, just like knowing a bunch of numbers won't help you unlock the lock. Even if you know the right numbers, you must know the correct order. Accuracy means the quality or state of being precise. Only by putting in the right numbers in the precise order will the lock unlock.

This lack of precision causes frustration. You have people who know a lot of information, yet still don't get the results they desire. There is nothing worse than knowing what you know, and it still *never* seems to be enough. A scripture found in 2 Timothy 3:7 states, *"Ever learning and never coming to the knowledge of the truth."*

Therefore, not only must you accept the laws that govern success, but you must be accurate in how you apply those laws in your situation. You don't need to know everything, but you do need to know some very specific things to succeed in your life. Think about it like this: if you are trying to hit a bull's eye with a dart, is it good for you to know everything outside of the bull's eye? You have even gone so far as to get multiple degrees and certifications about what lies outside of the bull's eye. And every time you throw the dart, you wonder why you miss, with all that you know? As opposed to focusing on the bull's eye, by putting all your energy into learning everything there is to know about the target you are trying to hit. Now, when you throw the dart, you are more likely to hit it.

This level of precision is what it takes to succeed. Accuracy demands that you not only know the right numbers for the lock but also be extremely precise in the sequence of how you enter them to unlock success in your life.

APPLICATION

This part is self-explanatory. After we established that you needed the combination (acceptance) and after I told you the right numbers in the right sequence (accuracy), I took the lock out of your hand and told you to open it without touching it. Sounds crazy, right? But what was I trying to imply?

None of what you know will do you any good if you don't apply what you know now.

It is always amazing to see someone who knows what to do, yet they are not doing what they know. I have repeated this notion several times already (and you will hear it plenty more), and you may think it is becoming redundant, but good, because I am really trying to drive that point home. Remember, repetition is the mother of all learning, and information is useless without application! Knowledge is not power in and of itself. Only through the application of that knowledge will you see the power evident in your life.

Lack of application is the same as trying to unlock a lock without touching it. If you don't apply yourself, then you can kiss goodbye to any hope of success!

THE COMBINATION TO SUCCESS

True success is locked up.

But this lock is not opened with a key, as is normally espoused.

I think the key to success is more like a combination lock, hence the example from earlier.

You typically hear about the "Keys to Success," but in some regards, I think that language can be misleading, because it encourages a person to think about an actual *key*.

Why does that matter, you ask? Well, the normal understanding of a key-type lock is that *you must have the key to open it.*

This may lead to some misunderstandings of the concept of success because people may feel that without this *"proverbial key,"* they can never be successful.

Do you see the problem with this school of thought? Unfortunately, this notion of a "Key to Success" can be easily (and I believe) misconstrued as an "actual key". When I say "actual key", I don't mean literal key or physical key. But it lends itself to the idea that success only comes to those who possess this "key". Without it, how can one ever succeed?

Consequently, this inspires excuses as to why some people have not achieved their greatness. They may even feel justified in making such an excuse because they can always say, "Well, I don't have the key." Even when asked how a person of similar circumstances, who came from a similar environment as them, succeeded, it is easier for them to respond, "They must have the key."

This "key" can mean a lot of different things, but most of the time, it is viewed as some sort of special advantage. At least, that is how it is normally looked at by non-achievers.

One of those proverbial "keys to success" is this concept of the "IT" Factor. I'm sure you have heard the saying "some people just have this thing called — It."

There is no real definition for "It," but one of the best descriptions I have found is this:

> The "It" factor is one of those undefined and subjective attributes that you either have or don't. And for those who don't have "It," this undeniable "It" factor is more than just an attractive quality... It's also a hallmark of success. And "It" falls into the category of you-know-it-when-you-see-it.[7]

This mode of thinking is easy for procrastinators, excuse makers, and people who do nothing to accept as truth.

The reality, though, is that there is a way to unlock wealth in your life, and that is by using a combination that can be universally applied to everybody.

---

[7] Wiskup, Mark. The It Factor and How to Get It: Becoming a Master Communicator. 2019, www.amanet.org/training/webcasts/the-it-factor-and-how-to-get-it-becoming-a-master-communicator.aspx

There are no "Keys to Success" as is commonly understood, and there is a *Combination*. Truly, the concept of a combination lock is an easier way to understand what success really takes. You already know success is not something easily attained.

The truth that most people don't want to accept is the fact that you must prove yourself worthy of success.

Now, when I say that there are those of you who will (automatically) try to disqualify yourselves & spout off about how or why you are unworthy.

But remember, we are learning how to go from being the wrong person to being the right person, so just keep reading.

Then there are others who will get all up in arms about undeserving lottery winners who got lucky, drug dealers/criminals who committed crimes and got rich, or cutthroat executives who used ruthless and deceptive business tactics for greed, etc. Let me remind you that ill-gotten gains (Proverbs 13:11a) will never last.

"Woe unto him that buildeth his house by unrighteousness, and his chambers by wrong; that useth his neighbour's service without wages, and giveth him not for his work; But thine eyes and thine heart are not but for thy covetousness, and for to shed innocent blood, and for oppression, and for violence, to do it. He shall be buried with the burial of an ass."
— Jeremiah 22:13, 17, 19

Remember in Joshua 1:8, God views success as either good success or bad success. I also established in the Preface that God will only release to the righteous. Well, if there is a lack of release in your life, then it stands to reason there must also be a lack of righteousness.

Let's think about that lock again. We know that if the right combination is input, the lock will open, and success will be released to you.

Exactly, what is that combination?

Wallace Wattles wrote a great book called *The Science of Getting Rich,* and in it, he stated, "The ownership of money and property comes as a result of doing things in a *certain way.*"[8]

Just like a simple combination lock requires three numbers to be input in a *certain* sequence to open, success requires three things, also done in a *certain* order.

ATTITUDE

"Attitude determines your limitation.
Meaning your belief system will determine how far you can go."
— **Dr. Myles Munroe**

Leadership Expert John Maxwell wrote in his book, *The Power of Attitude,* "You are only an attitude away from success."[9]

Attitude is the first part of the "Combination to Success," and this requires Acceptance.

Nothing great has ever been accomplished with a bad attitude. A defeatist, woe-is-me, cup-half-empty, every-day-is-gloomy, negative, pessimistic, Eeyore (from Winnie the Pooh) type of person has never achieved anything great.

What does having a "good attitude" mean anyway?

---

[8] Wattles, Wallace. The Science of Getting Rich. Abridged Edition. (Pennsylvania: Tremendous Life Books); page 10

[9] Maxwell, John. Book: The Power of Attitude. (Illinois: David C. Cook; 2001).

"In everything give thanks:
for this is the will of God in Christ Jesus concerning you."
— 1 Thessalonians 5:18

Looking at the scripture above, it is clear to see that God's will for your life is to have an "Attitude of Gratitude."

Now you might say, "What about all the hurt and pain in my life? How is it possible for me to be happy about that?"

Remember, I asked earlier what story you are telling yourself? Answer—Find the Good in It.

"And we know that all things work together for good to them that love God,
to them who are the called according to his purpose."
— Romans 8:28

This is what makes this "Attitude of Gratitude" possible because (in the end) all things work together for your good; therefore, be thankful in all things because *the joy of the Lord is your strength. (Nehemiah 8:10)*

In Acts 26:2, Paul says, *"I think myself happy."* This was while he was in shackles, standing in front of a man who could order his execution. To make a long story short, Paul ultimately was delivered from that situation.

Having a positive bent does not mean you don't see reality. Just because you are "positive" does not mean everything is positive. What I am talking about here is developing the ability to make the best of any situation. This begins with your "Attitude," and you must accept that.

An *"Attitude of Gratitude"* is where you start if you want to see any kind of meaningful change in your life.

Attitude Is A Decision

Having a good attitude is one of those things that everybody knows, but not everybody practices. Have you ever heard someone say, "This is just the way I am," as though they can't change? The truth is, they are that way because they decided to be. Your Attitude is totally changeable and controllable.

To have a certain attitude is to have a certain mindset. Deeper than just mere perspective, your attitude is literally your thought pattern. We will dive into mindset and how it applies to this philosophy in Chapter 6, "Mastering Your Mentality," but for now, I want to connect the dots between your mind and your attitude. To understand why, let's look at this Scripture;

> *"Let this mind be in you, which was also in Christ Jesus."*
> **— Philippians 2:5**

It would be easy to think that the most important words in this scripture are *"Mind"* and *"Jesus Christ,"* But I submit unto you that the most important word here is *"LET."* It is another way of saying "decide." The point of decision is always the catalyst for change, after which the rest of the scripture tells you exactly what you need to do to change.

You are not "just that way," as though there is no hope that you can't be different or better. But the power of Christ means the power to change. It simply begins with "how" and "what" you think. You are not stuck in your current situation as you might suppose.

I dare you to decide to think differently and take on a different attitude!

Attitude Affects Altitude

This maxim is quite popular, as I'm sure you have heard it before. Motivational speakers use it all the time. You see it hanging in office buildings in framed posters. But what does it really mean? The surface understanding states that a person's attitude will determine how high they go in life. But a more extensive study lets you know that this saying has a literal meaning and not just a practical one. I submit to you, it is the literal meaning that gives a person a greater comprehension of this truism's importance.

The saying, "Attitude determines your altitude," has its basis in aviation.[10] Airplanes are equipped with an "Attitude Indicator" (yes, it's a real thing) which measures the position of the nose of the plane in relation to the horizon. If the nose of the plane is pointed up, it is called "positive attitude." If the nose is pointed down, then it is called a "negative attitude."

Therefore, your "attitude determines your altitude." If the nose of the plane in relation to the horizon has a positive attitude, the plane rises. But if the nose of the plane is pointed downward in a "negative attitude" for too long without being corrected, the plane will crash and burn. What do you think happens to your life if you maintain a "negative attitude" for too long and don't correct it?

Attitude Awareness

Create your own internal "Attitude Indicator." Look at the direction of your life and its trajectory, then adjust accordingly to keep your attitude positive. Pay close attention to always having "Attitude Awareness."

Dr. Alan Zimmerman said in his book, *Pivot: How One Change in Attitude Can Lead to Success*, "I've noticed that attitude makes a huge difference in determining a person's level of success in life. In fact, attitude seems to make a bigger difference than age, sex, race, education, circumstance, or any other factor. Two people can have the same background and face the same situations, but experience very different outcomes. It's all about attitude."[11]

---

[10] Borden, Kit. What is the difference between altitude and attitude in aeronautics? Quora; January 29, 2018. www.quora.com/What-is-the-difference-between-altitude-and-attitude-in-aeronautics

[11] Zimmerman, Alan. Pivot: How One Change in Attitude Can Lead to Success (United Kingdom: Peak Performance Publishers); page 2

John Maxwell also said, "A good attitude does not guarantee success, but a bad attitude guarantees failure."[12]

Attitude is not the "be-all-end-all," but it is the first part of a combination that will guarantee success.

APTITUDE

Aptitude is the second part of the "Combination to Success," and this requires Accuracy.

This is one of those things that some people know and some people don't. How critically important your aptitude is to your success can not be emphasized enough.

The simplest definition of aptitude is: *your natural ability.* But, for our discussion, I want to expand on that definition just a bit:

Aptitude—is your God given ability to fulfill your purpose, by using your learned skills, natural talents, and spiritual gifts.

Your aptitude is how you have been specifically equipped with certain qualities to carry out your God-given assignment (Psalms 139:14). Therefore, use your uniqueness, because you have been equipped to excel.

> *"For as you know Him better,*
> *He will give you, through His great power,*
> *everything you need for living a truly good life:*
> *He even shares His own glory and His own goodness with us!"*
> **— 2 Peter 1:3 (TLB)**

---

[12] Maxwell, John. Attitude 101: What Every Leader Needs to Know (New York City: HarperCollins Publishers, LLC; 2003); page 4

Earlier, when we gave the scenario with the combination lock, the first thing we mentioned was acceptance. If the lock opens, you must accept that there is a certain way to get it open. To be successful, you must accept that there is a certain attitude you must decide to have to be successful.

The second thing we mentioned earlier was Accuracy. This is where aptitude comes into play. For the lock in our scenario, the numbers you input must be accurate, or else it will not open. Remember, our definition of aptitude is *"your God-given ability to fulfill your purpose by using your learned skills, natural talents, and spiritual gifts."*

What do I mean? Too many times, people believe that they are not successful because of something they don't have. This is simply not true. The problem is you are not using what you have, because you think it's not good enough. Nothing could be further from the truth.

Now, you may need to hone your skills or *perfect* your gift. Again, it is about you working with what you have, not wishing for what somebody else has. You are not successful because you have not accurately utilized your aptitude. Let me say that again:

> *You Are Not Successful Because You Have Not*
> *Accurately Utilized Your Aptitude!*

You don't need what anybody else has; you only need to use what you have!

It Takes Talent(s)

In the Bible, there is a story known as the "Parable of the Talents" (Matthew 25:14-30). I will not belabor going through the entire story verse by verse to give you a complete exegesis of the text, but I will give you a brief synopsis so that you have some context for the concept I am trying to point out here.

Jesus tells this parable to His disciples to show them the importance of both preparedness and productivity (both subjects of which we will talk about later in this book). To fully understand the truth Christ is revealing here, you must read Matthew chapters 24 through 26. But, for now, our focus is on this parable.

To literally make a long story short, Jesus says that there was a certain master who was about to take a journey and left a certain amount of talents with three servants. The amount of talents he gave to each servant was based upon that servant's ability (Matthew 25:15). It is important to note that the word "talent" in this story means money (we will see in just a bit why the word *"talent"* is strategic). The master then leaves for his journey, to return at some later, unknown date, having left no instructions on what each servant was to do with the talents that he gave them.

I should point out here that even though he did not give explicit instructions, there was still an expectation. The master gave the talents based on what he knew about each servant, and we will find out later in the story that, based on what the servants knew about the master, he expected them to do "something" with what he gave them.

So, the master gives five talents to the first servant, two talents to the second servant, and one talent to the third servant. The servant with five talents increased his to five more, the servant with two talents increased his to two more, and the servant with one talent hid his talent.

The master returned and asked each servant to give an account of what they did with what he left them. The one with five said, "I got five more for a total of ten." (Matthew 25:20) The one with two said, "I got two more for a total of four." (Matthew 25:22) The master gave the same reward to both: "Well done. You have been faithful over a few things, I will make you ruler over many things: enter into the joy of the Lord." (Matthew 25:21,23)

But the servant with one talent said, "I knew the type of man you were, so I hid my talent, and here is back the one talent you gave me." (Matthew 25:25) The master is clearly angered by this lack of productivity and calls the servant "wicked and slothful."

Side point: I want to reinforce what I was saying earlier regarding Proverbs 13:22, where I said the wealth (that is laid up) is not somebody else's, it is your wealth. You simply have to go from being one who was wicked, to one who is just. This servant had something that was laid up for him (the master gave him the talent to use, for increase), but because he didn't do what he was supposed to do, he didn't get what was intended to go to him and was considered wicked.

The master goes on to say that at the bare minimum, the servant could at least have done "something" with what he had, and not returned empty-handed by producing no **ROI**—Return On Investment. (Matthew 25:26-27)

The master tells his other servants to take the one talent and give it to the servant with ten, because *"for unto everyone that hath shall be given, and they shall have abundance: but from him which hath not shall be taken away even that which they have." (Matthew 25:29)* The master then says, *"Cast the unprofitable servant into outer darkness: there shall be weeping and gnashing of teeth." (Matthew 25:30).*

I realize, there is so much that I am leaving unexplained here, but the main point I want to make about this entire story and why it is applicable to aptitude is this: when Jesus told the parable, the word *"talent"* meant money. I said earlier this was strategic because God, in His infinite wisdom, knew that one day the word talent was going to have an entirely different meaning. Today, *talent* (as defined by Merriam-Webster) means "a special, often athletic, creative, or artistic aptitude. General intelligence or mental power. Ability: the natural endowments of a person."

If you mix the two—talent meaning money and talent meaning ability—with the story, you can clearly see that God gave you at least one (if not more) talent(s) that have value, and there are clearly consequences for either using or not using YOUR talent.

Now, before you go on some *"I-don't-have-anything-special-about-me"* tangent, hear this: the Bible said that the servant that hid their talent was considered wicked and slothful (Matthew 25:26). Remember earlier when I talked about the "wealth of the wicked" being "laid up" and I said it was not two different people, but it was the same person—I think this is further proof of that. Because I believe the master's anger was kindled by the fact that the servant could not see the *full* value in what the master left him.

Consequently, the master said, "You could have at least given people (i.e., the money changers) the opportunity to see the value of the talent I gave you and produce something with it." But you hid your talent and did nothing with it.

Here is the truth, plain and simple: inherent in every human being alive is God-given ability known as Aptitude. If there were a key to success, this would be it. You must tap into what is unique about you in order to succeed. This is why the master was so angry; the servant did not use the talent he was given. These talent(s) were gifts.

God has given you a gift(s). It is in your best interest to use it!

The Bible states:

> *"For the gifts and calling of God are without repentance."*
> **— Proverbs 18:16**

> *"A man's gift maketh room for him, and bringeth him before great men."*
> **— Romans 11:29**

Your greatness is manifested through your gift(s); therefore, grow in your gifting.

The reason aptitude is the second part of the combination to success is because you don't unlock the combination without using what God gave you. Just like you must accept that you must have the right attitude, you must also accurately utilize *your* aptitude. You must know the value of that which God gave you and not diminish it.

Your prosperity depends upon using your aptitude accurately.

ACTION

Action is the last part of the "Combination to Success," and this requires Application.

> *"You can't hire someone else to do your push-ups for you."*
> **— Jim Rohn**

You don't get your lock unlocked watching other people unlock theirs; YOU must act to unlock your lock.

If you remember from the scenario of the combination lock, the last thing I did was take the lock from you and say, "Open it."

Remember I said, "Think positive thoughts. Maybe it will come open. Try speaking to the lock—you know, 'name it and claim it, blab it and grab it.' Still won't open, huh?"

We ultimately concluded that while thinking positive thoughts and even stating positive affirmations with conviction are great, they will not make anything happen in your life by themselves.

Yes, you must accept having the right attitude and accurately utilize your aptitude, but lastly, you have to apply appropriate action.

> *"Even so faith, if it hath not works, is dead, being alone."*
> **— James 2:17**

You must *physically* grab the lock, and *physically* pull it open. Unfortunately, for too many people, this is where the Combination to Success breaks down.

Because they (or should I say, you) are not doing everything necessary to see success unlocked for you.

Let me be blunt: You are not taking the appropriate actions you know you should take to succeed!

Again, I reiterate, "you know what to do, you are not doing what you know."

This is the combination to unlock success and prosperity in your life:

Attitude + Aptitude + Action

Be, Do, Have!

GIVE TO GET

"For unto whomsoever much is given, of them shall be much required."
— Luke 12:48 (Emphasis added)

The size of your dream will determine what is demanded of you in return.

So, the question is, what are you willing to "Give" so that you can "Get"?

There is no Success without Sacrifice.

I know it is not easy, but nobody told you it would be. I know it is not convenient, but change has never been created through convenience.

Your dream will require more, take more, demand more of you than anything else in your life.

If you complain that it is inconvenient, then you will not be met with sympathy.

Those who have ever accomplished anything great were inspired by inconvenience.

To be clear, nothing that has been done on Earth that is worthwhile has ever been convenient. No, the fact that it was a challenge and an obstacle to be overcome is the force that continued to push the envelope to create real change.

In other words, the problem itself is what motivated a person of awesome achievement to find the solution.

One must go through adversity to achieve advancement, not avoid it. That is how a true impact on the earth is made.

Are you the kind of person who can have such an impact?

I say, YES, YOU ARE!

MPOWER ME

CHAPTER 3

The Principles of Prosperity

"There is nothing more powerful than a principle,
it is a divine law that cannot be broken."
— **Roger L. Daye**

"Money is plentiful for those who understand the simple
laws which govern its acquisition."
— **George S. Clason**

(Author of The Richest Man in Babylon)
"Teach them the statutes and the laws, and make known to them the way
in which they are to walk and the work they are to do."
— **Exodus 18:20 (NASB)**

LAWS OF THE LAND

Think back to when you were in science class, and you first heard about "scientific laws."

You may have had to learn the Laws of Motion, Laws of Physics, Laws of Chemistry, and so forth. To everything that existed on the earth, it appears that at some point in history, a scientific law was discovered about it. Here is a good explanation of scientific law by Anne Marie Helmenstine, Ph.D.:

*"A law in science is a generalized rule to explain a body of observations in the form of a verbal or mathematical statement. Scientific laws imply a cause and effect between the observed elements and must always apply under the same conditions. In order to be a scientific law, a statement must describe some aspect of the universe and be based on repeated experimental evidence. Scientific laws do not try to explain the 'why' the observed event happens, but only that the event actually occurs the same way over and over. A scientific law is sometimes called a **natural law.**"*[13]

One of the most well-known natural laws is the Law of Gravity—what goes up must come down. Gravity has always existed, even before it was discovered to be a law. It was in operation well before Sir Isaac Newton came along.

Now imagine, after you were told about this law and you were shown irrefutable evidence that it is a very real thing, you still say, "I don't believe it!"

Is your lack of belief going to stop the law from existing? Absolutely not, it is real, whether you believe it or not.

Let's say you don't know about this law; you have never heard of it. Does that stop it from existing? Absolutely not. It is real, whether you know about it or not.

There is a statement in the legal field that I want to point out here: "Ignorance is no excuse of the law." Just because you don't know about a law does not mean you won't suffer the consequences of breaking it.

Do you see my point here? The law is the law. There is a domain in which certain laws operate, and there is nothing we can do to change them.

---

[13] Helmenstine, Ph.D., Anne Marie. Last accessed 2018. https://www.thoughtco.com/definition-of-scientific-law-605643

Therefore, we must "Accept" them. There is that word again. Accepting that you need a positive attitude to succeed coincides with accepting that there are not only natural laws, but also laws that govern success.

PRINCIPLES OF PROSPERITY

Just like there are Laws of Science, there are also Laws of Success. Whether you knew that or not, whether you believe that or not, does not matter.

They exist.

I refer to these Laws as "Principles."

In a nutshell, a principle is simply defined as a fundamental fact.

I am using the words "laws and principles" interchangeably here. Earlier, when scientific law was explained, one of the things that had to be true for it to be considered a "Law" was that it had to occur the same way over and over. Principles can exist in a myriad of ways. There are principles of business, principles of human nature and psychology, and so on. But the most powerful principles are always Biblically based. You can bank on these as truth personified.

"That ye may be the children of your Father which is in heaven: for He maketh His sun to rise on the evil and on the good, and sendeth rain on the just and on the unjust."
— Matthew 5:45

"Then Peter opened his mouth, and said, of a truth I perceive that God is no respecter of persons: But in every nation he that feareth Him, and worketh righteousness, is accepted with Him."
— Acts 10:34-35

Here in these scriptures, you find the Power of Principles summed up.

No matter the person, place, predicament, or perspective, principles are equal (be it sun or rain) everywhere.

This is best captured in the saying, "God is no respecter of persons, but He is a respecter of principles."

SINNER or SAINT

Simply put, sinners or saints are the same when it comes to those who are putting the principles of prosperity into practice. You may struggle with that statement, but it is the truth anyhow. You may get mad at the fact that God is willing to bless a sinner over a saint, if they are using His principles, yet the saint is not. But which is worse, an ungodly person who is putting godly principles into practice, or a godly person who is not putting godly principles into practice?

Let's look at it this way: you have a scenario with two people. The first person is not in a relationship with God, but they are consistently using godly principles to govern their finances. They are using Biblical principles to start successful businesses. They are providing jobs for people, making charitable contributions, and having a community impact. (Luke 16:8)

Whereas the second person is in a relationship with God but will not consistently apply godly principles to their finances. They won't start a business, are not having a community impact, and are unwilling to make charitable contributions. (Luke 16:11)

Which one is God more likely to bless with wealth?

The above example really hits home when you think about it this way: the multi-million-dollar company you work for makes it a point to give away at least 10% of its profits annually to charitable causes, yet you struggle to give 10% of your paycheck to your own local church.

Then you get mad at the wealth of the unsaved CEO, who does apply this Biblical principle to his company's budget, while you (who *are* saved) still won't apply that one, simple, Biblical Principle to your personal finances.

God has made it plain: Principles He can trust, but People He cannot.

"Thus, saith the Lord; Cursed be the man that trusteth in man, and maketh flesh his arm, and whose heart departeth from the Lord. Blessed is the man that trusteth in the Lord, and whose hope the Lord is."
— Jeremiah 17:5, 7

Therefore, in His divine sovereignty, He has mandated that whoever practices His principles, that is, whom He will bless.

"The Lord maketh poor, and maketh rich: he bringeth low, and lifteth up."
— 1 Samuel 2:7

Do you get it?

Put the Principle into practice and you will have the Promise.

So, let us discover a few of these principles.

LAWS THAT GOVERN SUCCESS

Disclaimer: The laws I listed here are not in order of importance, as they are all equally valuable. Also, please understand that in no way is this an all-inclusive or exhaustive list.

"And there are also many other things which Jesus did,
the which, if they should be written every one, I suppose that even the world itself could not contain the books that should be written. Amen."
— John 21:25

In full disclosure, I have barely scratched the surface of this subject matter. I simply listed a mere fraction of the laws that I think can be of some use to you. In the hopes that it will show you how to recognize "the truths" applicable to your situation when you need them, because there are many.

Now let's get started.

Law of
POTENTIAL

"And Jacob was left alone; and there wrestled a man with him until the breaking of the day. And when he saw that he prevailed not against him, And he said, Let me go, for the day breaketh. And he said, I will not let thee go, except thou bless me. And he said unto him, What is thy name? And he said, Jacob. And he said, Thy name shall be called no more Jacob, but Israel: for as a prince hast thou power with God and with men, and hast prevailed."
— Genesis 32:24-28

Have you ever asked yourself the question, "Is this all I am"? The answer to that question is NO. The truth is, no matter where you are, **you can always be more, do more, and have more!** A thing can always change into its greater self—this is the Law of Potential. This simply means no matter what, it will be better. Why? Because there is always room for improvement. The depths of God are so deep and the heights of God so high that one can never feel like they have arrived, at least while still living. If we are alive, we are ever striving to go deeper and higher in Him. God will always show you who you can be.

Think about Jacob wrestling with what the Bible calls "a man." Some theologians say that it is not an angel that Jacob is wrestling with, but rather himself. Or I should say the person he could be. Why would he have to wrestle with himself and say, "I will not let you go until you bless me," you ask? Because there is something to be said for proving how bad you really want "it." To get this blessing, you must *be* something, and the proverbial wrestling is the proof that you are willing to make the sacrifice. *"And when he saw that he prevailed not,"* the blessing was released in the form of a new identity. *"What is your name"?* This is God's way of giving you awareness, so you can adjust. Growth is inevitable, but the critical factor is to be intentional about that growth, so you don't just get bigger, but you also get better. Expansion is the means of expression that you are more today than you were yesterday, and you can be more tomorrow than you are today.

Law of
PROGRESS

"In all thy ways acknowledge him, and he shall direct thy paths."
— **Proverbs 3:6**

"The steps of a good man are ordered by the Lord:
and he delighteth in his way."
— **Psalm 37:23**

"And we know that all things work together for good to them that love God,
to them who are the called according to his purpose."
— **Romans 8:28**

History has shown that things evolve naturally. Things move forward as time moves forward. Change is constant, whereas adaptation, alteration, and adjustment are not. Those unwilling to change will die. I'm not talking about a physical death but a death of far greater magnitude—the death of opportunity. Work with change instead of resisting it, and you can take advantage of every advancement of change.

This is an important law to note because it proves you do not have to *"stay stuck"* nor do you have to regress, because you can progress. How, you ask?

Simply put;

To focus forward, you must go God-ward (2 Cor. 3:4)— this is the Law of Progress.

"I will go before thee, and make the crooked places straight: I will break in pieces the gates of brass, and cut in sunder the bars of iron: And I will give thee the treasures of darkness, and hidden riches of secret places, that thou mayest know that I, the Lord, which call thee by thy name, am the God of Israel."
— Isaiah 45: 2-3

Law of
PROCESS

"For the earth bringeth forth fruit of herself;
first the blade, then the ear, after that the full corn in the ear."
— Mark 4:28

The Bible says, *"Let ALL Things be done decently and in order." (1 Corinthians 14:40)* This is a mandate from God that there be an "order" to things.

Process is defined as a series of actions, motions, or operations leading to some result. "Result" is the key term here. There is never a need for a process if you are not trying to reach some desired result. But God has clearly shown us the importance of process because God always has a desired result in mind. It is what I call a destination; it is where He wants you. Process is how He gets you there. Therefore, process is another way of saying direction.

Destination with no direction is confusion. And God is not the author of confusion, according to 1 Corinthians 14:33. Therefore, if there is confusion in your life, it could be that you lack direction, or should I say, you have not submitted to the process. Think about this whole chapter regarding principles; it really is just God's process at work. He established a structure whereby a certain outcome was "guaranteed" if the process was followed. To everything, God has put a process in place. Think about this scripture:

"Humble yourselves therefore under the mighty hand of God, that he may exalt you in due time: Casting all your care upon him; for He careth for you. But the God of all grace, who hath called us unto his eternal glory by Christ Jesus, after that ye have suffered a while, make you perfect, stablish, strengthen, settle you."
— 1 Peter 5:6-7, 10

Do you see the process? Beloved, if you find the process here, you will also find your prosperity.

"That He would grant you, according to the riches of His glory, to be strengthened with might by His Spirit in the inner man; That Christ may dwell in your hearts by faith; that ye, being rooted and grounded in love, May be able to comprehend with all saints what is the breadth, and length, and depth, and height; And to know the love of Christ, which passeth knowledge, that ye might be filled with all the fullness of God. Now unto Him that is able to do exceeding abundantly above all that we ask or think, according to the power that worketh in us."
— Ephesians 3:16-20

Put simply, He takes you through a process of perfection, which allows God to gradually grow you by taking you to higher heights and deeper depths. The idea here is that as you increase in your experiences with Him, He will release more and more to you to be used for His Glory!

The Combination of Success (Attitude + Aptitude + Action) is nothing more than a Process of Prosperity.

Law of
POSSESSION

"And I commanded you at that time, saying,
The Lord your God hath given you this land to possess it:
ye shall pass over armed before your brethren the children of Israel,
all that are meet for the war."
— Deuteronomy 3:18

You must *"Act as if"* you have what you want—*God has given you the land!*

Then, *"If you act,"* you will have what you want. *Now, go in and possess it!*

The Law of Possession very simply means taking what is rightfully yours. There are things that God has already given us that we have yet to possess. God essentially told the children of Israel, "It's yours now. **Go Get What I Have Given You."**

The Law of Possession requires you to take initiative. It will not just fall in your lap while you sit on your seat doing nothing. You must take the land. Why? Because God has given it to you. I wonder how much God has given you that you have yet to take.

Law of
PROPHECY

"And He said unto me, son of man, can these bones live?
And I answered, O Lord God, Thou knowest.
Again, He said unto me, Prophesy upon these bones, and say unto them,
O ye dry bones, hear the word of the Lord."
— Ezekiel 37:3-4

Your current reality is not the only reality, but by divine function, you can exist in a greater realm to live your authentic life. There is an abundant life available for you.

"I have come that they may have life, and that they may have it more abundantly."
— John 10:10 (NKJV)

I dare you to speak to your situation. No matter how dire your current circumstances are, they can change for the better—if you would but say so.

"Let the redeemed of the Lord say so."
— Psalm 107:2

"For by thy words thou shalt be justified, and by thy words thou shalt be condemned."
— **Matthew 12:37**

The Law of Prophecy includes the Principle of Proclamation.

"And calleth those things which be not as though they were."
— **Romans 4:17 (KJV)**

"Death and life are in the power of the tongue:
and they that love it shall eat the fruit thereof."
— **Proverbs 18:21**

It has been said that what you say is not as important as how you say it. When it comes to Proclamations (or more affectionately known as Affirmations), including and incorporating emotion is a critical part of making what you say effective.

Put differently, if you don't feel it when you say it, then say it until you feel it.

The research behind why this is important is amazing. It has been proven that emotionalizing your words in relation to affirmations makes what you say work.

In this instance, an affirmation is saying positive statements while thinking positive thoughts. The positive statements give direction to thoughts, which give destination to things.

This is where feeling/emotion comes into play. There must be inspiration with intention which gives way to invitation which creates interaction.

One of the greatest natural examples of the Law of Prophecy is when President John F. Kennedy prophesied that man would go to the moon. It was September 12, 1962, at Rice University in Houston, Texas, when he made the famous speech, and it was a prophecy to be sure. He famously said:

"We set sail on this new sea because there is new knowledge to be gained, and new rights to be won, and they must be won and used for the progress of all people..."

"We choose to go to the moon in this decade and do the other things, not because they were easy, but because they are hard, because that goal will serve to organize and measure the best of our energies and skills, because that challenge is one that we are willing to accept, one we are unwilling to postpone, and one which we intend to win, and the others, too.

"But if I were to say, my fellow citizens, that we shall send to the moon, 240,000 miles away from the control station in Houston, a giant rocket more than 300 feet tall, the length of this football field, made of new metal alloys, some of which have not yet been invented, capable of standing heat and stresses several times more than have ever been experienced, fitted together with a precision better than the finest watch, carrying all the equipment needed for propulsion, guidance, control, communications, food and survival, on an untried mission, to an unknown celestial body, and then return it safely to earth, re-entering the atmosphere at speeds of over 25,000 miles per hour, causing heat about half that of the temperature of the sun--almost as hot as it is here today--and do all this, and do it right, and do it first before this decade is out--then we must be bold.

"However, I think we're going to do it, and I think that we must pay what needs to be paid... But it will be done. And it will be done before the end of this decade."

I encourage you to listen to the speech in its entirety. It is a shining example of how to "speak those things that are not as though they were."

This prophecy of John F. Kennedy came to pass on July 16, 1969, at 10:59 p.m. Astronaut Neil Armstrong placed the first human foot onto an outer space celestial body and declared, "One small step for man, one giant leap for mankind."

I pray this inspires you to speak to your situation. Prophesy to your prosperity. Let me prophesy over you:

> *I prophesy that you will choose to be successful not because it is easy, but because it is hard. I prophesy over you that this goal of success will serve to organize and measure the best of your energies and skills. I know this challenge is one you are willing to accept and unwilling to postpone, one in which you will win!!!*

Law of
PERSPECTIVE

"And he answered, Fear not:
for they that be with us are more than they that be with them.
And Elisha prayed, and said, Lord,
*I pray thee, **open his eyes, that he may see.**"*
— 2 Kings 6:16-17

"If all you see is what you see you will never see all there is to be seen."
— Dr. Tony Evans

"Perspective is when you go from noWhere to now-Here."
— Wayne Dyer

In today's self-help society, it would be easy to confuse this Law with Visualization, which is defined as the formation of mental visual images. But Perspective is more powerful than just having vision because vision is about what you see (in the future tense), whereas perspective is about the way you see (present tense). If you have the wrong outlook in the present, you will have the wrong outcome in the future. Therefore, when one pictures something, if visualization is the formation, then perspective is the foundation for that formation.

The Law of Perspective most influences our self-image. In this instance, your perspective matters because it will answer the question: How do you see yourself?

You want to always "see yourself as the best version of yourself." Why? Because any image held in the mind, transfixed by faith, will manifest.

Repeat this aloud:

"The Me I See is the Me I will Be."

One of the greatest books I have ever read was *Psycho-Cybernetics* by Dr. Maxwell Maltz. His profound insights on self-image and the power thereof were life-changing for me. Dr. Maltz was a plastic surgeon who discovered the power of self-image via his interactions with his patients after surgery. He performed successful plastic surgery on people with birth defects, disfigurements from car or workplace accidents, or other conditions. He observed that, after removing hideous deformities and grotesque abnormalities to make them completely beautiful, some patients recognized the success of the surgery, appreciated their new appearance, and were extremely grateful. In those people, their confidence would skyrocket, and they would go on to accomplish great things. They had made excuses before because of the way they looked, but now they saw themselves as different and better.

But in other patients who received the exact same results, he noticed that after the scars from the surgery were healed and barely noticeable, their reaction was different. They still saw themselves as ugly or deformed, even though the ugliness of their defects was physically removed.

From these different reactions to the same result of a successful surgery, Dr. Maltz surmised that it had to be in their mind dictating how they saw themselves. He realized their perception of themselves did not come from the mirror; it came from their mentality. What they thought was there (or, in this case, not there) was more important than what actually was.

Dr. Maltz theorized that the mind was like a cybernetic device. In layman's terms, a cybernetic device is an automatic control system. The easiest example would be a thermostat in your house. Once you set the temperature on a thermostat, even when it fluctuates up or down, it will eventually return to its original setting.

Dr. Maltz found out that even though the surgery was a success, some people could not change their internal thermostat (i.e., their own self-image) to see themselves as new when he let them look in the mirror. They would fluctuate and go back to seeing themselves as the same. But it was all in their minds. He said that the mind was a psycho-cybernetic device, meaning it was a psychological, automatic control system that was a self-adjusting realization to always become what you see yourself as.

But what is wonderful is that he also knew that just like a physical thermostat, the setting could be changed, but only if one was intentional about shifting one's perspective. If you can see it, you can be it because "it" will be according to how you see it. You will always find what you're looking for, be it positive or negative.

I close with this truth: God's power is proportionate to your perspective.

We see this clearly in Ephesians 3:19, where it says, "**according to** the power that worketh in us." In other words, God can only move to the degree that you can see Him move.

If you change the way you look at things, then the things you look at will change.

Law of
PERSISTENCE

"You must be consistent with God,
and persistent with man."
— Jesse L Curney III
(Sr. Pastor, New Mercies Christian Church)

"And I say unto you, Ask, and it shall be given you;
seek, and ye shall find; knock, and it shall be opened unto you.
For everyone that asketh receiveth;
and he that seeketh findeth; and to him that knocketh it shall be opened."
— Luke 11:9-10

What does not exist because we do not persist? What would you have accomplished if you had not quit? How much greater would your life be if you had not given up?

There is a Law of Persistence that states if you keep going, you will get there. Even if you can't see how you will make it all the way through to the end, then go as far as you can, and you will see how to go further.

"Nothing in this world can take the place of persistence. Talent will not; nothing is more common than unsuccessful men with talent. Genius will not; unrewarded genius is almost a proverb. Education will not; the world is full of educated derelicts. Persistence and determination alone are omnipotent."
— Former U.S. President Calvin Coolidge

You can't have persistence without perseverance. While the words seem similar, they are not the same. Persistence is having a certain attitude, whereas perseverance is doing certain actions. Persistence is the attitude of a winner, and perseverance is the actions of a winner. Persistence says, "I will not be stopped," while perseverance is what gets you back up once you get knocked down.

Law of
PROVISION

"For the Lord God is a sun and shield:
the Lord will give grace and glory:
no good thing will he withhold from them that walk uprightly."
— Psalm 84:11

There is a Law of Provision that encompasses one's ability to Produce. God extends provision because He expects productivity. According to Genesis 1:28, being productive is literally His first mandate to man.

"And God blessed them, and God said unto them, Be fruitful, and multiply, and replenish the earth, and subdue it: and have dominion over the fish of the sea, and over the fowl of the air, and over every living thing that moveth upon the earth."
— Genesis 1:28

Productivity is the purpose for provision. There is no need for God to give anything to anybody who is not going to do more with it. Remember the parable of the talents? The master punished the servant not because he only had one talent but because he did not take his provision and be productive with it. Could it be that you are praying for God to make provision in your life, but the problem is that you have not shown Him how you will be productive with it? Once He gives the release, how will you make it increase?

Often, when we pray for God to provide, we are praying the prayer with the purpose of consuming whatever He gives us. God is not interested in giving you a fish; He is interested in teaching you how to fish. This is why He says, I gave you the power to get wealth. Imagine how some of our prayers sound to God:

Lord, give me the money to pay my bills. Lord, give me the money to buy this or that. Lord, give me the money to consume.

The consumption of the seed that God gives is why there is no harvest. God only gives because He expects you to do more with it. Show Him your plan for productivity, and I guarantee He will provide. God gives because He wants a return on His investment.

"Now he that ministereth seed to the sower both minister bread for your food, and multiply your seed sown, and increase the fruits of your righteousness."
— 2 Corinthians 9:10

Patience accompanies provision. But patience, as we see it here, is a character trait for growth, not an excuse to do nothing under the guise of, "I'm waiting on God."

"But let patience have her perfect work, that ye may be perfect and entire, wanting nothing."
— James 1:4

See the "wanting nothing" part? That is the provision. The next verse is how you get the provision.

"If any of you lack wisdom, let him ask of God, that giveth to all men liberally, and upbraideth not; and it shall be given him."
— James 1:5

The Law of Provision means that God will always provide for those who come to Him in faith with a plan.

"But let him ask in faith, nothing wavering. For he that wavereth is like a wave of the sea driven with the wind and tossed. For let not that man think that he shall receive any thing of the Lord. A double minded man is unstable in all his ways."
— James 1:6-8

Don't make belief a burden; believe until you behave like you believe, and God will bombard you with blessings.

"Now it shall be, if you diligently obey the LORD your God, being careful to do all His commandments which I command you today, the LORD your God will set you high above all the nations of the earth. All these blessings will come upon you and overtake you if you obey the LORD your God: Blessed shall you be in the city and blessed shall you be in the country. Blessed shall be the offspring of your body and the produce of your ground and the offspring of your beasts, the increase of your herd and the young of your flock. Blessed shall be your basket and your kneading bowl. Blessed shall you be when you come in and blessed shall you be when you go out."
— **Deuteronomy 28:1-6 (NASB)**

Law of
PROPORTION

Here is a law that God follows that you are probably familiar with, which is *Luke 12:48: "to whom much is given, much is required."*

This is the Law of Proportion.

This is where Uncle Ben's famous words of wisdom to Peter Parker (Spider-Man) came from: "With great power comes great responsibility."

The universe is proportionate in that way. Anything you desire or demand, something of equal value will be desired or demanded of you.

There is a misconception that if you take one step, then God will take two.

When the truth is, you get what you give.

If you take one step, God's one step is always bigger, but if you take two steps, God's two steps will be bigger still.

*"Now unto him that is able to do exceeding abundantly above all that we ask or think, **according to** the power that worketh in us."*
— **Ephesians 3:20 (Emphasis added)**

We love to leave off the part that says, *"according to the power that works in you."* This is another conditional clause.

There is always a part that you must play, and God said I will always meet you where you are. (James 4:8)

God has mandated this as law for the sole purpose of helping us understand we cannot expect what we did not earn.

This is the way this Law works.

"But this I say, He which soweth sparingly shall reap also sparingly; and he which soweth bountifully shall reap also bountifully. Every man according as he purposeth in his heart, so let him give; not grudgingly, or of necessity: for God loveth a cheerful giver. And God is able to make all grace abound toward you; that ye, always having all sufficiency in all things, may abound to every good work."
— 2 Corinthians 9:6-8

This is an important law to understand because it lets you know where you stand when you contribute. Too many times, we have false expectations of God. We tend to treat God as though He is our genie in a heavenly lamp. Prayer then becomes the proverbial rubbing of the lamp, and the life we picture is something we "wish" we could have.

Work hard so you never have to wish, because wishing never works.

What you put in is what you will get back out.

Proportion is defined as a balanced or pleasing arrangement. A harmonious relation of parts to the whole, with respect to magnitude, quantity, or degree. You must work with God with the understanding that God does not work for you. In other words, do your part and God will do His.

"Be not deceived; God is not mocked: for whatsoever a man soweth, that shall he also reap. For he that soweth to his flesh shall of the flesh reap corruption; but he

that soweth to the Spirit shall of the Spirit reap life everlasting. And let us not be weary in well doing: for in due season we shall reap, if we faint not."
— Galatians 6:7-9

Think about the advantage this gives you. If you understand this Law, then you must also understand that you are where you are based upon your own actions (or lack thereof).

You get out what you put in. It is proportionate.

If you don't like the results you are getting, the answer is not praying harder, fasting more, or blaming somebody or something else; simply correct what you are putting in and do the work.

With that being said, I don't want to imply that simply working harder is the answer in and of itself. I want you to understand that you must do the right work. (Remember, the last part of the Combination to Success was Action.)

You must grasp this truth: to get something of value, you must give something of value.

The greater the value you give, the greater the value you get. This is the Law of Proportion.

Law of
PREPARATION

"Therefore, be ye also ready."
— Matthew 24:44

How many opportunities are missed because we are not ready to take advantage of them when they come?

The Law of Preparation simply states, "The truest evidence of faith is preparation."

81

If you really believed in God, then you would get ready for it.

> *I once heard a story about a town that was suffering from a terrible drought. So, at the town hall meeting, the townspeople asked, "What are we going to do?" The mayor answered, "I cannot make it rain, because if I could, I would." Then someone came up with the idea to try one of those old Indian rain dances. What would it hurt? At this point, they were desperate to try anything. So, all the townspeople met on a certain day to pray and dance for rain. The entire town gathered in the town square, and one little elderly lady had an open umbrella over her head. The mayor asked her, "Ma'am, why do you have an umbrella; it has not rained in weeks?" She replied, "If you really believed God was going to send rain, then you would have brought an umbrella."*

That is preparation - proactive faith.

Preparation is your way of acting "as if" you are ready to receive the thing you desire to be released. If you know God is about to send your harvest, when is the best time to build the barn, before or after the harvest comes? There is Biblical precedent that suggests that the harvest will not come until the barn is built.

> *"And he said, thus saith the Lord, Make this valley full of ditches."*
> **— 2 Kings 3:16**

This scripture is an example of the Law of Preparation at work. In 2 Kings 3, the story is about three kings going to war. During the march to the enemy, they ran out of water. The situation looked bleak because they saw it as a sign that God was not with them. One of the kings asked, "Is there not a prophet here so we can enquire of the Lord?" They found a prophet of God named Elisha who prophesied that not only would God give them water, but He would also give them the victory over their enemy. But to get the water, they first had to dig ditches all around to catch the water for which they were believing. (Read the story in its entirety for yourself to get the full blessing.)

Do you see the moral of the story? They had to make things ready for the release. I am convinced that there are some preparations you need to make in your life before God will command an outpouring.

God's expectation is only for us to do what we can. He will ask a question like, *"What do you have in your house?"* (2 Kings 4:1-7) This was the question asked of the Widow of Zarephath. The Prophet told her to go and borrow pots and borrow not a few. It was not until the pots were in place that the oil began to flow. Do you have your pots ready? Are you prepared to prosper? Therefore, make ready the room for the release.

Law of
PHYSICAL HEALTH

"What? know ye not that your body is the temple of the Holy Ghost which is in you, which ye have of God, and ye are not your own? For ye are bought with a price: therefore, glorify God in your body, and in your spirit, which are God's."
— 1 Corinthians 6:19-20

The Bible refers to your body as "The Temple," which means it is critical that you understand the importance of taking care of your physical body.

Physical health is listed as a law here because it has been proven over and over that physical fitness has a direct impact on financial fitness. I'm sure you are saying that it takes more than just being physically healthy.

Well, yes, it does (and we will talk more about other forms of health in the coming pages). But the truth is that being healthy plays a vital part in being wealthy.

Think of the people whom you view as successful, and tell me how many of them take their health seriously. The answer is all of them, and I don't know who you thought about, but it does not take a rocket scientist to look around and realize that you just don't see that many out-of-shape millionaires.

This law was really brought to bear for me in a conversation I had with a friend of mine named Ms. Oretha Johnson. She said something that would have a profound effect on me regarding health. Ms. Oretha (who was in her mid-sixties) said, "If you look at Jesus, He was always on the move, healing people, performing miracles, and preaching or teaching the gospel. Imagine if Jesus were unhealthy and sick because of poor choices in exercise and diet, then He would be too overweight and out of shape to do what God called Him to do, with all the walking and movement going from place to place."

WOW, that was so true, but it was this statement that stuck with me the most: she said:

"You have to be able to go when God says go, Ministry requires Mobility!"

From that statement, I made a choice to change.

I did not want to complicate it. I knew the keys for me were commitment in diet and consistency with exercising.

When I say diet, I am not talking about some strict meal plan, I simply mean going for the better alternative and showing restraint when you know you are going too far. Therefore, I said I will stick to this simple strategy.

Moderation in my diet while choosing healthier options.

Then I said exercise requires four simple things:

1. Effort: Doing what must be done.
2. Excellence: Doing the very best you can. Don't cheat yourself.
3. Effective: Doing only the most productive things.
4. Endurance: Doing it until you get the results you desire.

The secret to each one is that it begins with "Doing." When it comes to physical health, there is no excuse. **GET IT DONE!**

Law of
PERSONALITY

"Examine yourselves, to see whether you are in the faith. Test yourselves.
Or do you not realize this about yourselves, that Jesus Christ is in you?
—unless indeed you fail to meet the test!"
— 2 Corinthians 13:5 (ESV)

Excerpt from *Psychology Today* called *The Science of Personality:*

"The human personality is a curious, multifaceted thing. Each person has a unique mix of characteristics, and individual values, as well as different traits in themselves and others.

Questions of personality have challenged humans from the dawn of personhood: Can people ever change? What is the difference between normal and pathological behavior? Do people perceive others the same way that those individuals perceive themselves?

Because personality is so pervasive and all-important, it presents a clinical paradox of sorts: It is hard to accurately assess one's own personality, yet impossible to overlook that of others. But since personality can make or break one's relationships at home and at work—and because each person aspires to be grounded in who they truly are—researchers will continue to dig deeper into why people are the way they are and how personality influences each individual's behavior."[14]

For a wonderful breakdown of "Personality" in general and the origins that constitute our understanding today, please feel free to visit **www.britannica.com/topic/personality**.

---

[14] The Science of Personality. Psychology Today. Last Accessed 2018.
https://www.psychologytoday.com/us/basics/personality

If you Google the definition of personality, this comes up: *The combination of characteristics or qualities that form an individual's distinctive character.*

The reason I included personality as a law is because it is a component that makes you uniquely you. Your personality is something you must accept; there is no escaping it, but there is always room for improvement.

Your personality is part of the reason you do things in a certain way. It is consistent in either helping us or hurting us, making us or breaking us, all the while most definitely molding us or misshaping us. Your personality includes your paradigm as well as your personal philosophy. It is the perch from which you sit, your internal culture.

I believe that many people live by the Shakespearian moniker, "To thine own self be true." This has gotten us into more trouble than I care to admit, because the "self" that we are being true to is often our "less self" rather than our "best self," with a this-is-just-the-way-I-am stance.

Juxtapose that with what scripture tells us: In 2 Corinthians 13:5, Paul said, "Examine thyself." Jesus said multiple times, "Deny thyself" (Matthew 16:24, Mark 8:34, Luke 9:23). As people, we tend to put ourselves on the throne of our lives rather than allowing Christ to assume this position.

I want to be clear here, it is extremely important that you be yourself because that is the only way you can succeed is through your aptitude; that is the special gift that God gave you, that only you can use. Albert Einstein once famously said, "In a world where you can be anything, be yourself." Dr. Seuss went on to say, "No one can be 'Youer' than you." So, I want you to understand it is essential you always be your distinct, unique, and special self. But, at the same time, understand you can grow by always making positive improvements in the areas you know you need it.

Therefore, use the Law of Personality to your advantage by going above and beyond your shortcomings and taking the properties that make *"you"* you and *bettering your best.*

Law of
PURPOSE

"Before I formed thee in the belly, I knew thee;
and before thou camest forth out of the womb I sanctified thee,
and I ordained thee a prophet unto the nations."
— Jeremiah 1:5

"For I know the thoughts that I think toward you, saith the Lord,
thoughts of peace, and not of evil, to give you an expected end.
Then shall ye call upon me, and ye shall go and pray unto me, and I will hearken
unto you.
And ye shall seek me, and find me, when ye shall search for me with all your heart."
— Jeremiah 29:11-13

"It is God himself who has made us what we are and given us new lives from Christ
Jesus;
and long ages ago he planned that we should spend these lives in helping others."
— Ephesians 2:10 (TLB)

We will continually talk about purpose and the different facets of it throughout this book. But first you must understand, there is a Law of Purpose and it comes in the form of intentionality. Intentionality is what makes you effective.

John Maxwell says in his book, *The 15 Invaluable Laws of Growth,* that the Law of Intentionality is the foundational law of growth.[15] Intentionality is like the

---

[15] Maxwell, John. Book: The 15 Invaluable Laws of Growth (New York City: Center Street, a division of Hachette Book Group, Inc., 2014); page: 9

scope on a gun. If you are going to hit your target, then you will have to be extremely intentional. What does this have to do with "Purpose," you ask?

Everything. I want to pose another question: Is it possible to be intentional without doing it on purpose, or is it possible to do something on purpose without being intentional? I rest my case. God was extremely intentional when He created you, and He created you on purpose, for a purpose, and with a purpose. You cannot see the good success He has in store for you outside of your Purpose. That is what makes it a Law that governs Success.

Purpose requires precision. Connect that statement to why *Accuracy* is part of that combination lock. Without precision and accuracy, you don't get the lock opened. The same goes for purpose: without using your purpose, you don't succeed to the degree that God designed.

Nothing is a coincidence, and there are no accidents; everything is done with intentionality. God's timing comes into play here. There is a certain specificity to things; nothing "just happens."

John O. Jones (my mentor) says that there is an absolute exactness to the things that we must decide to do. There is no ambiguity, there is no gray area, there is no maybe. It is Yes, or No.

Be precise. Don't be "wishy washy."

Life is not a game of checkers; it is a game of chess. If you don't know how to play chess, it behooves you to learn it. Just like life, it is a game of strategy, and the person with the best strategy wins. If victory is what you seek, the game forces you to make moves with a purpose.

By the time you finish reading this book; you will know how to "Find Your Purpose"!

Law of
PLACE

"Let not your heart be troubled: ye believe in God,
believe also in Me. In my Father's house are many mansions:
if it were not so, I would have told you.
I go to prepare a place for you."
— John 14:1-2

Have you ever felt "out of place"? As if you did not know exactly where you were supposed to be, but you knew this was not it. Like, there has to be a better "place" for me?

"The Lord God placed the man in the Garden of Eden to tend and watch over it."
— Genesis 2:15 (NLT)

"By faith Abraham, when he was called to go out into a place which he should after receive for an inheritance, obeyed; and he went out."
— Hebrews 11:8

After reading the scriptures above, do you get the point?

There absolutely is a PLACE for you!

A God-designed, God-destined place created specifically for you. Oftentimes, people feel as though "there is no place for me." Nothing could be further from the truth. This place could be geographical, relational, professional (meaning career), mental, emotional, physical, spiritual, and financial. These are some areas where you need to be in the right place.

Take inventory of your life and see "where" you are. There is an environment that God desires for you to thrive in every aspect of your life; any place outside of that place you can only at best survive.

Think fish out of water. There is a certain place it was made to be, and so were you. It behooves you to figure out where that place is and get there.

"Blessed is the man that trusteth in the Lord, and whose hope the Lord is. For he shall be as a tree planted by the waters, and that spreadeth out her roots by the river, and shall not see when heat cometh, but her leaf shall be green; and shall not be careful in the year of drought, neither shall cease from yielding fruit."
— Jeremiah 17:7-8

Earlier, we said that God expects productivity. Could it be that you are not producing because you are not planted? When you look at Palm Trees, Cactuses, Bamboo, Oak Trees, etc., they only grow when they are planted in the right place. The Law of Place means you can only prosper once you are planted in the proper place. Again, I reiterate this "place" is not always geographical. Sometimes "getting in the right place" simply means creating balance (Proverbs 11:1) in the different areas of your life.

I like to use a tool called the *"Wheel of Life"* when I'm coaching a client. It helps them see where they are possibly out of balance. The "Wheel of Life" is a diagram that contains eight sections that, together, represent one way of describing a whole life.

The sections are:

1. Spiritual
2. Relationships (i.e., Family)
3. Social Life (time with Friends, etc.)
4. Spouse (Significant Other)
5. Business/Career (to include Finances)
6. Recreation
7. Health (both Physical & Emotional)
8. Personal Growth/Development

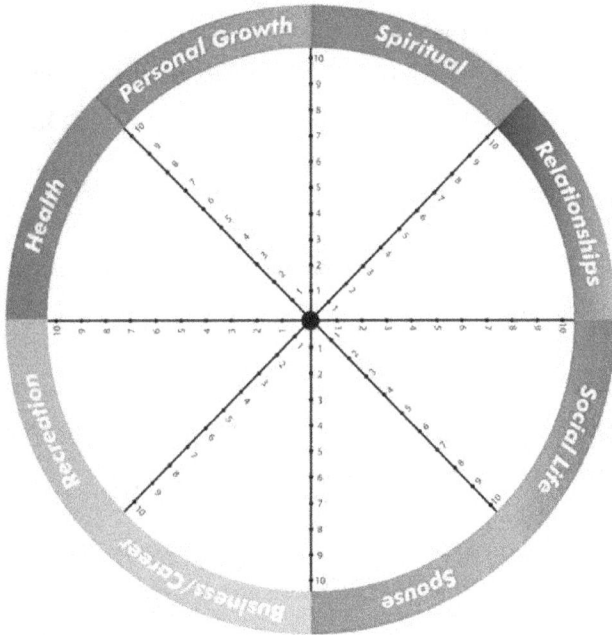

The diagram is a simple yet powerful tool for visualizing all areas of your life at once to see possible room for improvement. It can help you see where you are potentially out of place or not in the right place in your life. Visit www.mpower-me.info for a free download of a *Wheel of Life* template, along with instructions.

Take time to diligently seek God for every area of your life and see where He desires for you to be planted via prayer (Mark 9:29).

There is a place for you!

Law of
PROMOTION

"For promotion cometh neither from the east, nor from the west, nor from the south.
But God is the judge: he putteth down one, and setteth up another."
— **Psalm 75:6-7**

Promotion in the scripture above means "the desire for *self*-advancement." The idea is that anything you try to do in your own strength will inevitably be ineffective. In other words, trying to promote yourself won't work; it has to come from God.

What then qualifies you for promotion?

Remember, God is a respecter of principles. Therefore, the person who puts principles into practice positions themselves for promotion.

Absolutely, God wants you to have a Godly ambition, because advancement (in and of itself) is not bad. But, self-advancement (which is fueled by flesh) is futile, because you act as if you don't need God.

God desires to see you excel. But excelling in God only comes by operating with Excellence in Him. We will talk more about *Excellence* in Chapter 6, but for now, just know, excellence is committing yourself to "doing the very best you can, with what you have to work with" while in your present position, and in so doing God has promised to promote you.

Maintain humility, and you will see that there is always more available to you.

Position yourself for promotion.

Law of
PRIORITY

"But seek ye first the kingdom of God,
and His righteousness;
and all these things shall be added unto you."
— Matthew 6:33

The purpose of priority is for presence. I am talking specifically about God's Presence.

"Thou wilt shew me the path of life: in thy presence is fullness of joy; at thy right hand there are pleasures for evermore."
— Psalm 16:11

"Now the Lord is that Spirit: and where the Spirit of the Lord is, there is liberty."
— 2 Corinthians 3:17

You can accomplish so much more with God than you could ever hope to accomplish without Him (Romans 8:31). The old saints had a saying, "Only what you do for Christ will last." Why? Because...

"For it is God which worketh in you both to will and to do of his good pleasure."
— Philippians 2:13

Work with God to see true fulfillment happen in your life. According to Matthew 6:33, there is a pattern prevalent in that Scripture that goes like this:

1. Priority – *But seek ye First...* Make God the most important thing in your life.

2. Presence – *The Kingdom of God and His Righteousness...* He has promised that He will be with you. (Hebrews 13:6)

3. Prosperity – *And ALL these things will be added unto you.* He said that He will release blessings once you allow Him to assume that top spot.

The Law of Priority simply says to put God first and He will ensure you receive everything else you need.

Law of
PERMISSION

"For as many as are the promises of God, in Him they are yes; therefore, also through Him is our Amen to the glory of God through us."
— 2 Corinthians 1:20 (NASB)

After seeing the scripture I referenced above, I bet you're wondering why I did not call this the *Law of Promise*?

Well, the answer is really quite simple; while most people already believe they have the promise, the issue is that they don't feel they have *Permission*.

All the promises of God are:

Yes - God's pledge and commitment to bless you with what He desires for you to have. Just bear in mind the "Yes" here is predicated on you being in the Will of God.

Amen - which is defined as " It is So," this is your permission to go after what God said yes to. However, it is not permission to do whatever you want to do. (1 Corinthians 10:23)

Beloved, as long as God has given you a promise, that also means He has given you permission.

Tired of being rejected? Being denied? Being told, "no"? What if you give yourself permission to have what God wants you to have, instead of always putting your hope in someone else to meet your needs? As Christians, when we don't get what we want, we love to say, "I'm waiting on God," but what if God is waiting on you? Have you considered that any form of negative response is a manifestation of your own thoughts? What if, consciously, you want to hear yes, but subconsciously you are telling yourself, "no?" If whoever you are asking for permission is not giving you permission, it is because they don't have the authority to give it, and because you have not given it to yourself.

- You are granted permission to BE everything you were created to BE.
- You are granted permission to DO everything you were created to DO.
- You are granted permission to HAVE everything you were created to HAVE.

The Law of Permission very simply means: "Yes, You Can."

I've listed it as a law here because, if you are going after what God desires for you to have, then you have to have permission to do so. Your boldness and your confidence come from the fact that you are obeying God.

"And this is the confidence that we have in him, that, if we ask any thing according to his will, he heareth us: And if we know that he hears us, whatsoever we ask, we know that we have the petitions that we desired of him."
— 1 John 5:14-15

Permission has to do with positioning.

You can't be told "no" if you are in the right position to hear "yes."

If your will is positioned (*Rom 8:31*) with God's Will, you will hear "YES" every time.

You are granted permission.

POWER OF PRAYER

I could have talked about Prayer anywhere in this book, but it makes the most sense here in this chapter. However, I purposefully did not make "Prayer" a Law by itself; because ultimately it goes with "ALL" of the Laws!

While it is true that a lot has been said about the "Power of Prayer," it is also true, not enough can be said about it.

There are just not enough words for me to explain how critical "Prayer" is to Godly Success!

"Prayer is something everybody knows how to do, but not everybody does it.
...Lord, Teach us to Pray..."
— Luke 11:1

It is mandatory that you pray on how to incorporate all of these *Laws* into your life, as you will have to remain prayerful in order to see proof of any of these "Principles of Prosperity" happen for you.

Prayer is where we upload our issues, and God downloads His instructions.

Our connection to Him comes through this form of communication.

Jesus said in John 8:32, *"And ye shall know the truth, and the truth shall make you free."*

I submit unto you that the truth of these *Laws* will be realized through prayer, and this will bring about freedom; therefore, you must remain vigilant to seek Him, committedly, consistently, and continually.

> *"Seek ye the Lord while He may be found,*
> *call ye upon Him while He is near"*
> **— Isaiah 55:6**

> *"But without faith it is impossible to please Him:*
> *for he that cometh to God must believe that He is,*
> *and that He is a rewarder of them that diligently seek Him."*
> **— Hebrews 11:6**

Prayer happens in three ways...

- Literal
- Actual
- Perpetual

Luke 18:1 *"Men ought to always pray and not faint."*

- Literal prayer is the intentional prayers that we pray that are purposeful.
- These intentional, purposeful prayers are committed ones.
- Prayer is always needed.

Matthew 6:9-13 *"...Give us this day our daily bread..."*

- Actual prayers are the intermittent prayers that we pray that are practical.
- These intermittent, practical prayers are consistent prayers.
- Prayer is a necessity.

1 Thes. 5:17 *"Pray without ceasing."*

- Perpetual prayer is the internal prayer that permeates our soul.
- These internal, permeating prayers are continual prayers.
- Prayer should never stop.

I told you about the Law of Persistence. Well, here is one of the main places where that persistence needs to be applied.

We have all heard the saying, "Prayer Changes Things," but I would submit to you that it is the persistence of your prayer that changes things. Why? Because only persistent prayer proves profitable. The Bible states in James 5:16, *"The effectual fervent prayer of a righteous man availeth much."*

ATTRACTION

You can't write a chapter on laws that govern success and not mention the popular "Law of Attraction."

The Law of Attraction was popularized by a book and movie called *The Secret*. What the movie lacked was the clear Biblical principles that made the Law of Attraction work.

The Law of Attraction works via alignment through actions, making attraction a consequence of action.

Conversely, the lack of attraction is a consequence of a lack of action.

This is the truth behind "Be, Do, Have." What bridges the gap between your being and your having is your doing.

The Scripture that I think most embodies this principle is *Mark 4:22-29*:

> *"For there is nothing hid, which shall not be manifested; neither was anything kept secret, but that it should come abroad. If any man have ears to hear, let him hear. And he said unto them, Take heed what ye hear: with what measure ye mete, it shall be measured to you: and unto you that hear shall more be given. For he that hath, to him shall be given: and he that hath not, from him shall be taken even that which he hath. And he said, So is the kingdom of God, as if a man should cast seed into the ground; And should sleep, and rise night and day, and the seed should spring and grow up, he knoweth not how. For the earth bringeth forth fruit of herself; first the blade, then the ear, after that the full corn in the ear. But when the fruit is brought forth, immediately he putteth in the sickle, because the harvest is come."*

Here, Jesus lays it out clearly:

- ❖ You must "Be" a certain type of person (verses 22-25)
- ❖ "Doing" certain things (verses 26-27)
- ❖ To "Have" (i.e., attract) a harvest (verse 28-29)

To me, this is the "Law of Attraction."

Remember, we mentioned earlier Napoleon Hill's statement from his book, *Think and Grow Rich*, he coined a phrase that for a lot of people has been a game-changer. It certainly was for me. He said, "Thoughts are Things."[16]

---

[16] Hill, Napoleon. Think and Grow Rich (New York: Skyhorse; 2016); page 19

I have seen the movie *The Secret*,[17] and I know they say this law originated from Wallace Wattles' *The Science of Getting Rich*. But in my opinion, the truest embodiment of the Law of Attraction is, "thoughts truly do *become* things."

Why do I say that, you ask? Because of one word in the phrase, and that is *"Become."*

Pardon my English here, but thoughts say who you "Be" and therefore things "Come."

Remember: "You attract what you are"!

Too often, people try to *become* better instead of just *being* better. It is like "Yoda" from the movie, *Star Wars,* said, "There is no try. There is either do or not do."

William Shakespeare wrote in Hamlet, "To be or not to be, that is the question."[18]

The truth is— it is about BEing, not BEcoming.

You must *Be* something before you can become it.

If you develop the mindset, you have already attained that which you are trying to attract. And while you are on your way to it, it is on its way to you.

If you *Be*, "it" comes. Work on BEing, not becoming.

But what about progressive development into something, you ask? That's why he said, "Thoughts are things."

---

[17] History of the Secret. Last accessed 2018; https://www.thesecret.tv/about/history-of-the-secret/

[18] Shakespeare, William. Hamlet. (New York City: Simon & Schuster Paperbacks; 2003); page 127

BEing begins in your mind. Think of the person who wants to become a doctor. Mentally, they must be a doctor in their mind first to eventually become a doctor in their reality.

So, you *be it,* then *become it.*

You don't become it, then be it. "Begin with the end in mind," said Stephen Covey, author of *The 7 Habits of Highly Effective People.*[19]

Energy flows where attention goes. This is the beginning of the "Law of Attraction." Attention (BEing) creates attainment via attraction (Becoming), but attention without action will not yield attraction.

THE PARADIGMS OF PROSPERITY

Remember when I said in the beginning that wealth is more than "mere money," well, this is one of the facets I was talking about.

Typically, we only focus on the money aspect of prosperity, but I want to point out a couple of others here.

> *"Beloved, I wish above all things that thou mayest **prosper** and be in health, even as thy soul prospereth."*
> **— 3 John 1:2**

The scripture above proves God has a very holistic idea of prosperity described by what I call the 3 Levels of Prosperity.

Level 1 – Wealth
Level 2 – Health
Level 3 – Sense of Self

---

[19] Covey, Stephen. Book: The 7 Habits of Highly Effective People. (New York City: Simon & Schuster; 2013); page 102

Your life falls into three Paradigms of Wealth, Health, and Sense of Self.

I put them as levels because most of the time, when prosperity is mentioned, we only scratch at the surface (which is just the tip of the iceberg) of its true meaning, but it does go deeper.

> Level 1 Prosperity is Wealth; God desires for you to be wealthy; this is a fact the Bible is very clear about. Therefore, there should be no shame in striving to get what God wants you to have.

> Level 2 Prosperity is Health; earlier, I listed it as a law, but I want to expound on that a bit to say it is in all capacities, in every area of your life. This is so you can enjoy the wealth that God blesses you with. You must be healthy— physically, mentally, emotionally, spiritually, relationally, and financially.

> Level 3 Prosperity is a Sense of Self. The scripture mentioned above says, "Even as your soul prospers." The word *"Soul"* here is translated in the Greek as vital life force, the seat of feelings, desires, affections, and aversions, one's will, intellect, and emotions. This is what I like to call a "Sense of Self," which is the essence of your being.

It is important to note that the Levels of Prosperity in this scripture have a "conditional clause"—"*EVEN AS*". This really reverses this passage, so truthfully it could be stated that once you **MASTER** (*we will talk about this in Chapter 5*) your Sense of Self and you have Health, then you get Wealth.

BLESSING BLOCKERS

There are things that prevent prosperity. You may also know them as "Blessing Blockers," but these are not snares set by some fowler. Unfortunately, most of the time, it is a trap of our own undoing. Truthfully, when it comes to a lot of our *"bad luck,"* we are falling into a pit we dug.

The P.I.T. that I am referring to is the "Prosperity Interrupting Temptations" that present themselves while going towards your destiny. They stop you from getting what God desires you to have. Be careful to avoid them at all costs.

Do not fall into the P.I.T of...

- ❖ *Poverty* – It is a mindset that says you are comfortable with lack.

- ❖ *Pain* – When you allow emotional damage and baggage to keep you in an unhealthy place. You do need to take some time to heal! But you cannot get stuck in "trying" to heal. Because life is going on with or without you, whether you are hurting or not. At some point, your pity party must end.

- ❖ *Pride* – making the vain mistake of thinking you don't need anyone else, and you have all the answers and can do it all by yourself.

- ❖ *Procrastination* – Don't be comfortable being comfortable. The reward of action is always greater than the risk of inaction.

- ❖ *Problems* – Being in love with the struggle to the point that it consumes you, and all you see is what's wrong and why it won't work.

- ❖ *Perfection* – Paying "pseudo" attention to unimportant details in what looks like an effort to be better, when really it is another form of procrastination that either stems from fear or laziness. It is not about being perfect; it is about being done, because perfect never gets done. Perfection can cause analysis paralysis. There's a fine line between doing it right and getting it done...

  To the best of your ability, "do it right," but more importantly, "get it done"!

- ❖ *Price* – Lack of money is a myth that seems like a good excuse not to move. Never allow cost to block your resourcefulness and creativity.

- ❖ *Pleasure* – Doing only what feels good. No pain, no gain.

Do not fall into these pits because they are only designed to distract, disrupt, and destroy by wasting your time, your talent, and your treasure.

ACCEPTANCE, ACCURACY, APPLICATION

My objective is simply to make you aware that not only are there laws that govern success that you must accept, but to caution you that if you do not accurately apply these laws, you will not be successful.

I want to share the term "Praxis" with you. Praxis is where theory meets practice. Imagine a large "X" with theory on one axis and practice on the other. The point at which they intersect and cross is where we want to remain closest. It is here that we are in a constant state of learning and doing.

These laws are enacted once **belief becomes behavior**. Therefore, don't just know them, but DO them. Because according to James 1:22, knowing the principle is not enough; putting it into practice is what's most essential.

For a free downloadable version of these laws, please visit **www.mpower-me.info**

MPOWER ME

CHAPTER 4

Why Sit We Here Until We Die?

*"Nothing happens until the pain of remaining the same
outweighs the pain of change."*
— **Arthur Burt**

*"You can't go back and change the beginning,
but you can start where you are
and change the ending."*
— **C.S. Lewis**

*"**Why** sit we here until we die?
They know that we be hungry."*
— **2 Kings 7:3,14 (emphasis added)**

There will come a time when we are all forced to face the painful question of "WHY"?

Why are you not successful? Why are you not wealthy? Why haven't you made more of yourself? Why have you not gotten it done yet? Why have you not started? Why are you procrastinating? Why are you so fearful? Why are you lying to yourself? Why do you keep making excuses?

Why, Why, Why...?

Your response to these critical questions will dictate whether you are doomed to live an average life or destined to live an abundant life.

WISHING WON'T WORK

Are you guilty of wishing for a better life? Wishing that things would just work out? Wishing somebody would just put a check in your hand to solve all your problems? Man, how great would it be to just win the lottery? If I had all that money, I would do the right thing with it. Why can't somebody help me?

Wishing, wishing, wishing...

Wishing is a form of fiction. It is unreal. Wishing will never make your dreams come true, but God will respond to what you do by faith. If you are going to move, then you will have to move by faith, for that is the only thing that pleases God (Hebrews 11:6). Faith is the evidence that says you can, when everything outside of faith offers evidence that you can't. Faith is the knowledge within the heart beyond the reach of proof (Hebrews 11:1).

FIX YOUR FAITH

"Even so faith, if it hath not works, is dead, being alone."
— James 2:17

❖ If your faith does not change how you function, you will never see what you believe come to fruition.

❖ Belief must become behavior to become a blessing.

Often, we determine the way God blesses us more than He does if we meet certain criteria. The question you must ask yourself is, are you qualified to be blessed? According to Psalms 1:1-3, if I meet the spiritual qualifications for the blessing, then the Bible clearly says, "Whatsoever I do will prosper." A lot of times, we don't connect the part we must play in making our miracles happen. Notice how the Jordan River did not part until the children of Israel stepped into the water first (Joshua 3:13). Notice Jesus did not call Lazarus forth until they moved the stone away (John 11:39-43). Therefore, the Bible says faith without works is dead (James 2:17). There is work that you must do to show your faith is real.

THE FAITH FIGHT

"But I need something more! For if I know the law but still can't keep it, and if the power of sin within me keeps sabotaging my best intentions, I obviously need help! I realize that I don't have what it takes. I can will it, but I can't do it. I decide to do good, but I don't really do it; I decide not to do bad, but then I do it anyway. My decisions, such as they are, don't result in actions. Something has gone wrong deep within me and gets the better of me every time."
— Romans 7:17-20 (MSG)

At one point in my life, my problem was that I knew a lot, but I didn't do a lot.

If the truth be told, I was not hungry enough.

Despite the monumental problems going on around me, both in my family and in my business, I wrapped my inaction in fear disguised as needing to know more before I decided to act.

I was ever learning, but never coming to the knowledge of the truth (2 Timothy 3:7).

Have you ever been there? Ignorantly wrapping your unwillingness to work in a willingness to wait in a futile attempt to say you can't do more until you know more.

All the while, the truth is, if you get started, then you can figure it out along the way.

"It is the start that stops most people."
— **Don Shula (Hall of Fame Coach)**

There is no perfect time. You can't wait until it's exactly right before you start; you must start, then make it exactly right.

HOW HUNGRY ARE YOU?

Zig Ziglar once said, "People who are unable or unwilling to motivate themselves and create hunger must be content with a life of mediocrity, no matter how impressive their talents."

Bob Harrison (aka Dr. Increase) went on to say, "Hunger is the root of change. All change involves discomfort, but if you are hungry enough, you can overcome this discomfort."

Your lack of happiness, hope, health, healing, and so on must create a hunger in you for change. Don't you want better, don't you want more? I know the answer, but what is your action? If I may speak candidly: your situation is far too dire for you to sit idly by and do nothing to change it.

"Why sit we here until we die" is another way of demanding, you have got to get up and do something about it.

The great Les Brown put it plainly when he said, "You gotta be Hungry." Your hunger creates a drive in you to get off the seat-of-do-nothing and go make it happen. John Maxwell said, "Dreams don't work unless you do." No dream will ever come true until you wake up and get to work on it.

MOVE FROM NO-THING TO EVERY-THING

There are two types of people in this world: those who are *doing something* and those who are *about to do something*. Which one are you? The choice is yours. Truthfully, only one type of person gets anything done, and that is those who are doing something. It seems that those who are *about* to do something never actually get around to doing it.

If something is going to happen, it will be because *you made it happen*! There is a barrier between **vision** and **manifestation,** or **idea** and **reality**. To break through that barrier requires the right kind of work.

You must go from doing **no**-thing right, to doing **some**-thing right, to doing **every**-thing right.

Now I know how that sounds, but let me qualify that statement.

I really mean every "right" thing. It is you doing all the "right" things to fix what is wrong in your life.

No, you may not be able to do everything right, but you know the right things to do that you have left undone.

This is less about perfection & more about pursuit.

Doing every "right" thing is defined as one right action built upon another and another. Again, not perfect, but right for what you are trying to achieve.

Stop giving up, stop giving in, stop giving out, stop throwing up your hands, and stop throwing in the towel. Unfortunately, we quit too quickly. Typically, we cash it all in right at the time it gets the hardest, as though it is too much to bear, not knowing that is precisely the point where we are right on the brink of breakthrough. Do you not know that the darkest hour is just before the break of day? I know it seems like a lot, I know it is not easy, but nobody told you it would be. Believe me, there is far too much riding on you succeeding for you to quit. Come hell or high water, find a way to get it done.

Think of the impact you will make, the influence you will have, and the inspiration you will instill in others to go after their dreams. Think of the lives you will change when you are successful. This is about a lot more than just you here. The most selfish act you can do at this point is not to do all you can to succeed.

MAKE IT MATTER

Be, Do, Have.

Who you are, what you do, and what you get in this life must matter to you!

Here are three areas where you have to make it matter more;

Mindset Matters

We will do a deeper dive into this subject in Chapter 6, but I want to briefly mention it here in the things that matter, because:

❖ "Mindset Matters Most."

   In your *"Pursuit of Prosperity,"* there are a lot of critical things that matter, but nothing is more important than your mindset.

❖ "Mindset Motivates Best."

   There is no greater force to motivate you to move than your own mindset.

❖ "Mindset Manifests Greatness."

   It was Napoleon Hill who said, "What the mind of man can conceive and believe, the mind can achieve."[20] Manifestation in your life begins with your mindset. Your greatness or lack thereof is wholly

---

[20] Hill, Napoleon. What the Mind Can Conceive, believe & Achieve. October 19, 2007. https://www.youtube.com/watch?v=2hA-7aq6OXI

dependent upon your ability to think greater, so you can see greater. In order to change your life, you must first change your mind.

Motivation Matters

Remember when I said only purity leads to prosperity? Well, this is where it applies. Your motivation comes from your motives. The word "motivation" is defined as the reason(s) one has for acting or behaving in a particular way. It goes on to say that motivation is the general desire or willingness of someone to do something. In other words, motivation is really your *"motive for action."*

How do you overcome chronic procrastination? The answer is "right motivation." You must give yourself a BIG enough carrot to go after. Incentive increases initiative, so prioritize your prosperity. Priority dictates matters of importance. If your prosperity is marginally important, but not the most important, then you won't prioritize it to actually get the things done necessary to achieve it.

Therein lies the question: What is your "WHY"? What forces you to fight for a favored future? What is your motive for action (i.e., motivation)? The "why" you do it will always carry more weight than "what" you do. Because if you don't have a strong enough "WHY" that you feel, then you will always feel like—why?

Why bother, why try, why go after it? Until you have a compelling enough reason to take massive action, you will not do everything in your power to succeed.

Movement Matters

"The actions necessary to start a thing
is always greater than
the actions necessary to sustain a thing."
— **Roger Daye**

The truth is, you will never finish if you don't start. Most people will never see success because of a failure to get started. You must shift your thinking; you would rather be the person trying to stop, instead of the person trying to get started. It has been said that motion is better than meditation. In other words, you don't get things done by just thinking; you only get things done by doing.

When you know you should do it but just don't feel like it then "act your way into feeling rather than feel your way into acting."

Ralph Waldo Emerson said, "Do the thing and you will have the power."

Movement matters, so get going. If you are doing nothing, then nothing gets done. Only action leads to accomplishment.

YOU "CAN DO" IT

Do you have a "can do" attitude? That means an attitude to do what you "can do." Don't allow self-imposed limitations to limit you from all the possibilities for you.

"For if there be first a willing mind, it is accepted according to that a man hath, and
not according to that he hath not."
— **2 Corinthians 8:12**

There are things you can do and there are things you can't do. Unfortunately, we love to focus on the things we can't do, whereas God "only" focuses on what we can do. No matter how large the obstacle or how big the problem, or the size of the adversity we face, we love to give God our lists of "can not's," when God only cares about our "cans."

In Exodus 2-4, we find the introduction of Moses. Please read those three chapters of Exodus in their entirety to get a full understanding of the interesting story of how Moses came on the scene. I will not spend a lot of time here other than to point out this scripture:

> *"And the anger of the Lord was kindled against Moses."*
> **— Exodus 4:14**

Moses was a man whom God used greatly, but he did not get off to the greatest start:

❖ His life began in an identity crisis: Even though he was a Hebrew, he was raised in the palace, because of a decree sent out by Pharaoh (the king of Egypt) that all male Hebrew children be drowned in the Nile River when born. Moses' mother saved his life by literally sending him up the creek without a paddle, so to speak. She put him in a basket after hiding him for three months and set him adrift in the Nile River, where he was found by Pharaoh's daughter, who raised him as her own son until he was forty years old.

❖ Then he suffered a crisis: One day, Moses saw an Egyptian beating a Hebrew slave, and when he intervened, the Egyptian was inadvertently killed. Moses thought that the incident was a secret, but it was later exposed, and this sent him into exile. For the next forty years of his life, he lived in the desert.

❖ Where he experienced an ignorance crisis: The Bible says one day he came upon a burning bush, which was not uncommon in the hot desert heat. What was strange was that the bush was continuously burning and not consumed. This caught his attention, and upon closer inspection, when he approached the bush, the voice of God spoke to him out of it. He could not understand how this could be (ignorance).

❖ Which then led to an instruction crisis: Moses had a conversation with this voice from the burning bush, which he accepted as the Voice of God. He proceeded to let Moses know that there was something that He needed him to do. Moses went back and forth with God, trying to explain why he was the wrong man for the job. This leads us to the scripture from earlier.

"And the anger of the Lord was kindled against Moses."
— Exodus 4:14

The problem was that Moses was only giving God "excuses" for why he could not do the job assigned to him. When he saw that the excuses were unsuccessful, he switched to reasons. People somehow believe that reasons are more legitimate than excuses (not true). There is no excuse for the reasons you give and no reason for the excuses you give for why you can't do what God says you can. This is what ultimately angered God.

Our excuses do not excuse us from doing what God knows we can do, even if we don't believe them ourselves. Consequently, His question to us after our myriad of excuses/reasons is simply, "What is in your hand?" (Exodus 4:2)

"Do what you can, with what you have, from where you are."
— Arthur Ashe

God does not make mistakes. He would not have called you unless He knew that you were capable. As a matter of fact, the calling is proof of the capability.

LEVELS OF ABILITY

Do you know you have three levels of ability? Depending upon the activity, these abilities are:

1. Things you "know" you can do.
2. Things you "think" you can do.
3. Things you "wish" you can do.

You can be poor at something, be okay at something, or be the best at something. Where do you believe you should put all your effort?

Success initially comes from strengthening your strengths (think "sharpening your saw").

There are things you know you can do—those are the things on which you should focus. Hone your skills and get better at them.

The ability to wish you could do something will never create meaningful change. The ability to think about doing something at a later time, once things get better, results in frustration because that time will never come if you keep thinking about it. Only by using your ability to do the things you know you can do (right now), that is what will change your situation.

The things you think you can do and wish you could do are not where you should put your energy.

THE CHALLENGE TO CHANGE

Change helps us to fulfill our destiny. If God desires for us to become aware of our need for change, then we must acknowledge that need by giving our full attention to ensuring that the change takes place. In God, it is always for our good.

Awareness → Acknowledgement → Attention

This is the process through which change takes place in your life.

Awareness

You cannot change what you do not know needs to be changed. Are there areas of your life that God is trying to show you that need improvement?

The answer is "YES"!

Your first step in the right direction is eliminating "Unconscious Incompetence." This is where unawareness lives. Ignorance is *not* bliss, as the cliché goes—what you don't know *can* hurt you.

For the purposes of understanding the different levels of consciousness, I have included the "Conscious Competence Learning Model[21]:

---

[21] Sinclair, Seth. How Do Adults Learn? Last accessed 2018, http://sinclairadvisorygroup.blogspot.com/2014/11/how-do-adults-learn-why-does-it-matter.html

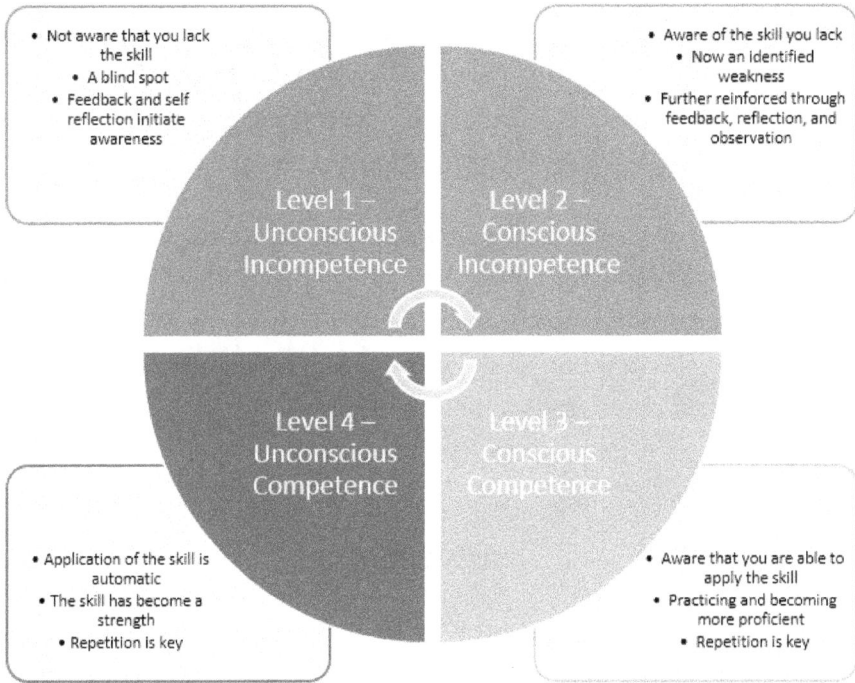

- Not aware that you lack the skill
  - A blind spot
  - Feedback and self reflection initiate awareness

Level 1 – Unconscious Incompetence

- Aware of the skill you lack
  - Now an identified weakness
  - Further reinforced through feedback, reflection, and observation

Level 2 – Conscious Incompetence

Level 4 – Unconscious Competence

Level 3 – Conscious Competence

- Application of the skill is automatic
- The skill has become a strength
- Repetition is key

- Aware that you are able to apply the skill
- Practicing and becoming more proficient
- Repetition is key

Acknowledgement

The importance of embracing change is critical to growth. God cares more about our character than our convenience. He wants you to know the consequences of your choices, be they good or bad. As a result, He will use whatever is necessary to get you to see your blind spots.

"But the God of all grace, who hath called us unto his eternal glory by Christ Jesus,
after that ye have suffered a while, *make you perfect, stablish,*
strengthen, settle you."
1 Peter 5:10 (Emphasis added)

Do you know that you need to change? Challenges come to change us. God will use crisis, calamity, and chaos as circumstances in your life to create a consciousness of change.

I am only able to tell you this because I personally know this process all too well. I know what it is like to not know what you don't know (Unconscious Incompetence). In those times, this is not a good place to be, because it seems like everyone else knows what you need to do except you.

Facing yourself in this area takes complete and total honesty and maturity. Ask yourself, have you done something different than what God wants you to do? Be honest with yourself, seriously. If the answer is "Yes," then you need to change. I know you don't like to hear that. Neither did I, but like I said earlier, only purity leads to prosperity. In this instance, this isn't even about personal gain; it is about peace of mind.

Attention

God uses situations to strengthen us. As the cliché goes, no pain, no gain. Go past your problems into your possibilities! Results are the reward for those willing to take risks. Give it your full and undivided attention because God will only respond to your faith in action.

God will make a way somehow. Here is where you need to TRUST the LORD.

Steps to change your situation:

- ❖ **Speak to create the atmosphere.** Begin stating emphatic affirmations of the desired direction you want to see your life go. (Mark 11:23)

- ❖ **Write to create accountability.** Create a checklist for change. Plan your work, then work your plan. (Habakkuk 2:2)

- ❖ **Apply to create accomplishment.** You must be committed to change. Acknowledge it, attempt it, achieve it. If you fail, accept it and adjust it. Then TRY AGAIN! Nothing is accomplished without action! (2 Corinthians 8:11)

CHANGED!

"So, all of us who have had that veil removed can see and reflect the glory of the Lord. And the Lord—who is the Spirit—makes us more and more like Him as we are changed into His glorious image."
— 2 Corinthians 3:18 (NLT)

One of the points I shared earlier was, "Change helps us to fulfill our destiny." It PRESSES us out of our comfort zone, PUSHES us to our personal best, and PULLS us to our next level. If we fail to embrace change, then our circumstances, our challenges, and the complexities of our personal and professional life will never change. Change is necessary and inevitable. We can initiate it and change for the better or life itself will drive us to it.

START AT THE FINISH LINE

Some people have the **faith** to take action. Some people have the **focus** to take action. Some people have the **fortitude** to take action. Then there are those who are **forced** to take action.

Those who are forced to take action means that the actions you are forced to take may not always lead to the success you are seeking. Why? Because if circumstances are such that you are "forced to take action," then you are being "reactive." Reaction is not the best action in terms of achievement, because it leaves too much to chance, whereas faith, focus, and fortitude, by contrast, are "proactive."

Pro-action is always better than reaction. Better stated, if you stay proactive, then you will not have to be reactive. Ask yourself which is better—being ready or getting ready? Well, if you stay ready, then you will not have to get ready (Matthew 24:44). It is the difference between starting at the finish line (proactive) or being finished at the start line (reactive).

Reaction says that no planning and no preparation intensifies the problem. When something happens that you are not ready for, the situation is made worse. Pro-action says prior planning and preparation prevent poor performance. We have all heard the saying, "People don't plan to fail; they fail to plan." I say, "Prepare to fail, because you failed to prepare."

You need both planning and preparation. Preparation without planning is like driving to a destination with no directions—this will always result in disaster. Planning without preparation is like directions to a destination, but no way to drive there. Planning with preparation means not only do you have a roadmap, but you also have a means and mode of travel to put in place.

ACTIVITY vs. PRODUCTIVITY

Unfortunately, too many people confuse activity with productivity. Being busy just to be busy never results in a blessing—it only becomes a burden.

You must know the difference between "Business and Busyness." One requires you to say "I," whereas the other requires you to say "Y."

Business spelled with "I" stands for inclusion and intentionality! In other words, I must be involved in the process for me to be productive. I must do everything on purpose, through purpose, for purpose, and with purpose. Again, nothing just happens. It only occurs when you make it happen. Your involvement matters. You must be present to win.

Busyness spelled with a "y" is lively, but meaningless activity in futility that forces you to ask yourself, "Why"? Never waste energy doing things where you cannot show what you did after you're done doing it. Do not confuse work with busyness. "Work" works. If it is not working, then you are just busy. You are not actually producing anything. If you are just busy being busy, then why are you doing it? Answer: We do not like to admit when it is not working.

Jesus said in *John 21:5, "Children, have ye any meat"*? Because I can see you are busy, but is it working? No. Well, "cast your nets on the right side of the ship." Only purposeful action leads to accomplishment, but pseudo-activity leads to aggravation.

Most people struggle with productivity because they deal with procrastination. It is not always about laziness (although some would argue [and maybe justifiably so] that procrastination is laziness in another form, though I digress). Procrastination says, "Do it later and suffer for it," whereas productivity says, "Do it now and see the benefits of it." While those benefits may not always be immediate, they are always definite. In contrast, procrastination has never failed to make us suffer.

THE ACHIEVEMENT GAP

Close the achievement gap.

Now, I do understand there is a contentious history with this term regarding academics, but I am not trying to get a moral or political debate started as it relates to the disparities in our country's educational system (although they are blatantly apparent).

No, I am saying to close the achievement gaps in your life. My definition of this proverbial gap is simple: *any areas of your life with unaccomplished goals create a gap.* If where you are and where you want to be are different, then my friend, that is an "Achievement Gap."

There are three steps to achievement:

1. Being - the present choice to embody your best self now
2. Doing - actions predicated upon the new you
3. Having - the manifestation of your transformation

Let's revisit the concept of *"Be, Do, Have"* — you cannot have without doing, and you cannot do without being. There are some things you want to do that you need to get started on. There are also other things you started on that you have yet to finish. These are your gaps. Start what you need to start, finish what you need to finish. Be, Do, and Have everything God has designed for you to Be, Do, and Have. From this point forward, say this out loud and let it be your mantra:

"I Can, I Will, I Must..."

- ❖ I Can Be More,
- ❖ I Will Do More,
- ❖ I Must Have More.

> *"Success is the result of the work you put in."*
> — **Lebron James (NBA Star)**

ESCAPE VELOCITY

In physics, escape velocity is the minimum speed needed for an object to "break free" from the gravitational attraction of a massive body.

It takes 60% of the fuel in the tanks of a rocket ship to get it to launch, and the other 40% to get it to the moon.

The idea behind taking massive action comes into play here. You maximize the moment by mobilizing momentum to not just get moving but keep moving.

Everything is on the line. You were built for this. It is time for you to take off. Here is where you give it ALL you got!!

If you are ever going to get a breakthrough, here is where the word comes to full fruition. You must literally "break through." For a rocket ship to break through the Earth's atmosphere, it must build up speed quickly, and this requires the greatest amount of resources and is also the most dangerous time of the launch. This is where things can go wrong all at once.

"What do you do when efforts have been applied,
but expectations have been denied?"
— **Bishop T.D. Jakes**

Try again. Do not quit. You don't give up; you get up, grow up, and go up. This is your chance, this is your shot, and it is time for you to launch!

All resistance, no matter what it looks like, is what will produce results (as long as you keep fighting through it). It doesn't matter if you're trying to build a brand, a business, or your body; you have to be able to overcome the resistance that happens when your new identity bumps up against your old identity.

Be prepared for setbacks, mishaps, mistakes, delays, denials, rejection, headaches, heartaches, and heartbreaks, things not working out, utter disappointment, and failure.

Well-meaning people (some who care about you and some who don't) will tell you that your idea won't work. Some will even say your plan is flat-out stupid. Do not be dismayed or discouraged. ALL these things are nothing more than the resistant forces and gravitational pull to keep you stuck where you are. They are designed to make you think your efforts are futile. This is nothing more than the "weed-out effect," for those who are not worthy of success cannot break free from such things to keep their eyes focused on the prize and not let anything stop them. After a while, they begin to believe these negative things. They procrastinate. They make excuses, and ultimately, they self-sabotage their own success.

But you are not of that number! You can see it is possible. You can see that other people suffered the same setbacks. Yet they not only survived, they thrived. They made it, and so will you!

As I am approaching the end of this chapter, you also are approaching the end of a chapter in your life. I leave you with these words to encourage you.

"Because of this decision we don't evaluate people by what they have or how they look. We looked at the Messiah that way once and got it all wrong, as you know. We certainly don't look at him that way anymore. Now we look inside, and what we see is that anyone united with the Messiah gets a fresh start, is created new. The old life is gone; a new life begins!"
— 2 Corinthians 5:16-17 (MSG)

MPOWER ME

CHAPTER 5

You Have Been M.P.O.W.E.R.-ed

"The key to Success is Self-Mastery."
— Dr. Cindy Trimm
(Speaker, Author, and Advocate)

Empower is a common term I am sure you are familiar with. The accepted definition is "to give a person (or persons) official power, to endow or enable one with authority".

I took that term and thought, How can one empower themselves?

The answer I came up with was *"MASTERY"*!

But, not just mastery of anything; it is mastery of what is unique to YOU.

This becomes the ultimate way for one to be *empowered* to walk out their destiny and fulfill their purpose.

PURSUE PURPOSE

I want to *Prove* that *People* can *Prosper* through *Perfection* of *Purpose*.

Often, people feel lost in life because they think they don't know their purpose. I want to liberate you today, because once you finish reading this book, you will be well acquainted with your purpose. I know I spoke about the *Law of Purpose* in Chapter 3, and we will dive even deeper into Purpose in Chapter 11.

But one has to look no further than the Book of Genesis to find that a major part of that purpose is to fulfill what God said in the beginning; His first commandment to man was to be *"fruitful and multiply"* (Genesis 1:28), which is very simply translated as "Growing and Giving."

As people, we are all commanded to *grow and give* of ourselves to make the world a greater place. You do that by using your gift(s) to make your contribution to the earth; that's why it matters that you are here.

You are designed and destined to dominate! And as long as you still have breath in your body, it is not too late for you to fulfill your purpose.

> *"He hath shown thee, O man, what is good:*
> *and what doth the Lord require of thee*
> *but to do justly and to love mercy, and to walk humbly with thy God?"*
> **— Micah 6:8**

At the end of your life, you want to be able to say *"YES"* to these 3 questions...

1. Did I Live?
2. Did I Lead?
3. Did I leave a Legacy?

The way you *Live, Lead,* and leave a *Legacy* is to BE, DO, and HAVE all that you are capable of Being, Doing, and Having through MASTERY.

Typical definition of Mastery is:

Knowledge and skill that allows you to do, use, or understand something very well; to have complete control of something

Remember you are "**Mastering Your Purpose,**" so with the above definition in mind, I simply add to it the MPOWER Definition:

Mastery means you are Being, Doing, and Having ALL you were created to Be, Do, and Have.

WHY "MASTERY"

*"And if a man also strive for **masteries**,*
yet is he not crowned, except he strive lawfully."
— 2 Timothy 2:5

The scripture above is the cornerstone of this entire philosophy.

Here is how I arrived at the conclusion that *"Mastery"* was the be-all-end-all.

I was at a place where I was putting in blood, sweat, and tears in different businesses and endeavors, going after different opportunities. All in an effort to succeed, but none of which worked.

In a fit of frustration, I cried out to God and said, "WHY?" And this is the scripture God brought me to: with tears in my eyes, I read this scripture and understood exactly why things were not working.

The reason why is because I was not *"striving lawfully."*

Remember the three scriptures I said earlier, which all had *conditional clauses*?

- Joshua 1:8
- Psalms 1:1-3
- 3 John 1:2

Well, *"Lawful"* is the conditional clause that explains them all.

Let's revisit them, but you need to read them in this order;

*"Beloved, I wish above all things that thou mayest prosper and be in health, **even as** thy soul prospereth."*
— 3 John 1:2

*"This book of the law shall not depart out of thy mouth; but thou shalt meditate therein day and night, that thou mayest observe to do according to all that is written therein: for **then** thou shalt make thy way prosperous, and **then** thou shalt have good success."*
— Joshua 1:8

"Blessed is the man that walketh not in the counsel of the ungodly, nor standeth in the way of sinners, nor sitteth in the seat of the scornful. But his delight is in the Law of the Lord; and in His Law doth he meditate day and night. And he shall be like a tree planted by the rivers of water, that bringeth forth his fruit in his season; his leaf also shall not wither; and whatsoever he doeth shall prosper."
— Psalm 1:1-3

You see, when God put these scriptures in this order for me, it became very clear that God was essentially saying, "I want you to succeed, worse than you want to be successful," but you have to do it in the right way.

❖ 3 John 1:2

The question becomes, how do you get your soul (Sense of Self) to prosper?

❖ Joshua 1:8

Success is the speaking, thinking, and doing of God's Word.

❖ Psalms 1:1-3

You are blessed when you forego doing it the world's way (which is what I was doing) and you commit (be planted) to doing it the

Word's way (the Law), after which *WHATSOEVER* you do will prosper.

Success felt as though no matter what I did, it was locked away from me.

That's when God took me to Proverbs 13:22 and showed me that the success that was *"Laid Up"* was not someone else's, but it was my own.

I had to go from being *Wicked* (one striving unlawfully) to being a person who was *Just* (one striving lawfully).

At this point, God told me, *"Roger, you do not know the Combination to Success!"*

Then He proceeded to explain to me everything that you have been reading in this book thus far and what you will continue to read about.

Beloved, when you strive for anything (i.e., trying to *Master* it) in this life, you have to do it the right way (lawful), because that is the only way you can be crowned.

M.P.O.W.E.R ME

In the next three chapters, I want to introduce you to the way of life known as **MPOWER**. I will mention each element of it here in this chapter, so you will know what to expect.

I cannot do a deep dive into each component of MPOWER (that will have to wait for another book), but I will explain it enough for you to get a firm grasp of how it will be beneficial to you.

"M.P.O.W.E.R" is the proprietary mechanism I use to teach a process that gives you a practical means to utilize the "Combination of Success".

Let me connect the dots for you—remember the scenario with the combination lock in Chapter 2?

We established that you have to *Accept* to open this lock; there is something you must first know— i.e., the combination.

Secondly, not just any random information would work. The combination had to be *Accurately* input.

Lastly, knowing the combination and the right order of the combination does not matter a whole lot if you don't *Apply* that knowledge to the lock. You have to physically do something to get the lock to open.

These three critical factors of Acceptance, Accuracy, and Application were all regarding the lock itself.

Remember, we said the lock represented success.

1. Acceptance: You must accept that there are specific laws that govern success.
2. Accuracy: Success requires knowing how to operate within these laws accurately.
3. Application: Using the Laws of Success to your Advantage.

Then we dove into what the actual combination to that lock (success) was.

Attitude + Aptitude + Action

This is the combination to unlock success in your life.

The first part of the combination is that you must accept that you must have a good attitude to be successful. The way you change your attitude is by **Elevating your Mind.**

Accurately using your Aptitude is the second part of the combination. Aptitude is a person's natural ability, you must **"Educate yourself on Methods"** as it relates to using your natural abilities (gifts) to get what God desires for you to have (remember the Parable of the Talents).

The last part of the combination is the Application of Action. This action means you must *"Evaluate your Model,"* therefore, see what other successful people have done to get to where you want to be and simply do what they've done (while still remaining true to you). Many have said "success leaves clues," and you can always duplicate success (because God is no respecter of persons, but He is a respecter of principles).

What is "M.P.O.W.E.R"?

- ❖ *Mastery* means striving to be, do, and have ALL you were created to be, do, and have. It is the process of continual and intentional growth and gain. The old slogan for Lexus (a luxury car manufacturer) comes to mind here: "The Relentless Pursuit of Perfection."

- ❖ This philosophy applies universally to ALL *People.* As an individual, you must find what you must Master that is unique and distinct to you.

- ❖ There is no Obstacle, Obstruction, or Opponent that cannot be *Overcome* through Mastery.

- ❖ *"With"* is a critical contingency that connects the "why" to the "what" and the "who."

- ❖ *Education*: the gaining of specific knowledge or "know-how" to succeed in any endeavor.

- ❖ *Resources*: available means, source of supply, and support to be utilized to help you accomplish your goals. Your Resources will come from resilient ingenuity by being resourceful.

MPOWER is a unique concept that allows a person to overcome challenges in Life, Leadership, and Legacy through a systematic "MPOWER Approach." The aim is to equip you with the tools necessary to be successful in all your endeavors.

I created MPOWER as a foundational framework that is fundamental to your success.

The idea here was to give you something you could use time and time again to achieve accomplishments, create change, and realize results.

The benefits of MPOWER are that it prepares, positions, and puts you on the path to prosperity. From there, you can walk out your destiny, knowing how to take it upon yourself to get what you need along the way.

Now, let's do a small recap: First, we laid a framework in which Acceptance, Accuracy, and Application were the standards that gave order to each piece of the combination.

That combination (Attitude + Aptitude + Action) becomes the structure through which you can see success.

The issue with the "Combination to Success" is that it is a bit abstract, meaning it is general in theory "attitude, aptitude, action." To tell someone that is all you need to succeed is like telling someone exercising and eating right is all you need to lose weight.

The natural question that follows is—how?

MPOWER transitions you from theory to practice.

MPOWER has three core components: Elevate Your Mind, Educate Yourself on Methods, and Evaluate Your Model.

Each component is designed to be a practical means to utilize the "combination" to unlock success in your life.

Acceptance	Attitude	Elevate Your Mind
Accuracy	Aptitude	Educate Yourself on Methods
Application	Action	Evaluate Your Model

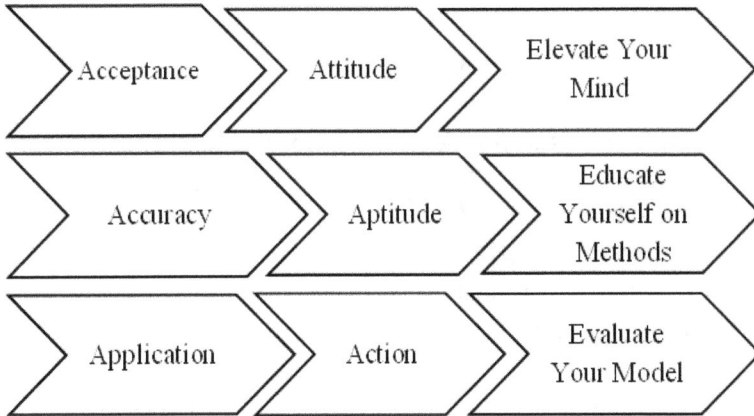

The different components of MPOWER break down to coincide with each part of the combination. I will briefly touch on the components to each area of focus for you to be successful.

I. Elevate Your Mind – Master Your Mentality

    A. Foundation of Faith (God's Promise for you)

        1. Attitude – can you deal with the disappointments? (i.e., remain positive, while handling the negative)

    B. Self-Discovery

        1. Improvement – you must ask yourself Who am I now, and how can I be better?

        2. Life – Do you have the character to persevere?

    C. Work on your Self – this is your personal excellence.

        1. See yourself as a success

II. Educate Yourself on Methods – Master Your Methodology

    A. Fundamentals (God's plan for you)

        1. Aptitude – can you develop the dos and don'ts?

    B. Self-Development

        1. Intellect – you must ask yourself, what don't I know, and how can I learn it?

        2. Leadership – Do you have the competence to perform?

    C. Work on your Skills – this is your professional expertise

        1. Study your way to success

III. Evaluate Your Model – Master Your Modality

    A. Function (God's Path for you)

        1. Actions – can you deliver?

    B. Self-Discipline

        1. Implementation – You must ask yourself, What am I doing that I should stop doing? What am I not doing that I should start doing?

        2. Legacy – Do you have the capacity to produce?

    C. Work on your Service – this is your profitable execution.

        1. Serve your way to success.

If successful people do what unsuccessful people are not willing to do, then MPOWER will help you "Develop the Discipline of Doing" in these three areas of Mastery:

Mentality > Methodology > Modality

*"But the God of all grace, who hath called us unto his eternal glory by Christ Jesus, after that ye have suffered a while, make you **perfect, stablish, strengthen, settle** you."*
— 1 Peter 5:10 (Emphasis added)

❖ Perfect = Mastery
❖ Stablish = Mentality
❖ Strengthen = Methodology
❖ Settle = Modality

Lastly, God brought me to 1 Peter 5:10, and He said this is how you will leverage your Mastery in your Life, Leadership, and Legacy.

The "suffering" you have been going through has all been a "Process of Perfecting."

By *Growing* through what you are *Going* through (*"after you have suffered a while"*); this is where you make the shift.

In order to see prosperity, you have to shift from struggle, scarcity, and survival (constant states of stress through suffering); being in these states' frames everything in your life (remember your life falls into the paradigm of wealth, health, and sense of self) to Significance, Strength, and Success.

Now let's go deeper as to how we do this.

MPOWER ME

CHAPTER 6

Master Your Mentality

"There is nothing either good or bad but thinking makes it so."
— **William Shakespeare (Hamlet)**

*"We cannot solve our problems with the same level of thinking
we used when we created them."*
— **Albert Einstein**

ELEVATE YOUR MIND

Let me say this plainly and boldly: GET YOUR MIND RIGHT!

Mastering your Mentality is a critical first step as it relates to success and achievement, because your mindset is the catalyst for all growth and change.

Here it is put plainly: "Your Mind Matters!"

We briefly touched on this in Chapter 4, now let's go a bit deeper.

It is crucial that you know your mind matters, because it alone will dictate how you "mind matters." Whatever you are dealing with, going through, and have or will experience, either past, present, or future, is predicated on thought, more specifically, your thought(s).

Life (literally) follows your lead.

Life is not happening to you; rather, life is happening through you.

Think about that for a moment, then think about the things that are (or are not) taking place in your life. Who is responsible? Unfortunately, we as people don't like to admit the part we play, especially when things are not going well.

"Does your environment influence your thinking
or does your thinking influence your environment?
To truly change is to think greater than your environment."
— **Dr. Joe Dispenza**

One of the laws that governs success is the *Law of Personality*, which creates your personal reality.

Let that sink in.

If that is the case, there is good news: If it ends with you, then it begins with you, and if it begins with you, then it also ends with you." In other words, if you broke it, you can fix it; truthfully, even if you didn't break your life, you can still fix it. The solution is simple in either instance; all you must do is be the change you want to see. This requires a paradigm shift.

"Your life rises to the level of your thinking."
— **Dr. Myles Munroe**

You begin the process of change by "Elevating your Mind."

Literally, you must start thinking on another level. When Jesus gave John a new revelation, it looked like this:

"After this, I looked, and, behold, a door was opened in heaven: and the first voice
*which I heard was as it were of a trumpet talking with me; which said, **Come up***
***hither, and I will shew thee things which must be hereafter.**"*
— **Revelation 4:1 (emphasis added)**

Now we know that John did not physically go, but he elevated his consciousness. He was commanded to "come up" to another level, and he did it through thought. Once he elevated his mind to another level, the scripture says, "I will show thee things." Imagine what you are not seeing because of low-level, shallow thinking. We'll talk about this a great deal in Chapter 10, but this is why Jesus told Peter to "launch out into the deep." (Luke 5:4)

Don't keep your view small by thinking small, but "launch out."

> *"And there came one of the seven angels… and talked with me,*
> *saying unto me, Come hither; I will shew unto thee."*
> **— Revelation 17:1 (emphasis added)**

This tells me that John made the leap. *"Come up hither"* is followed by *"Come hither."*

Beloved, if you trust God and take that leap of faith, the possibilities for you are endless.

In the first scripture, we read, "Come up hither and I will show thee." In the second scripture, we find, "Come hither and I will show thee." What's the difference? It's like watching a commercial and they say, "Let us *show you,*" your dream vacation, versus stepping off the plane and you already know this is going to be a thousand times greater than that commercial said. They greet you with the greatest welcome ever, grab your hand, and say, "Let us *show you.*"

It is one thing to imagine how great it would be to go, and it's another thing entirely to feel how great it is to arrive. The difference is entertaining the possibility versus experiencing the place. Therefore, elevate your mind to look beyond where you are so you can have the "greater" awaiting you.

WHAT IS THE "MIND"?

We think in pictures. When most people think of the "mind," they picture a brain. But that is the equivalent of thinking about a car and only picturing the engine. The mind is no more just the brain than a car is just the engine. Clearly, we know a lot more goes into making an actual car than just the engine. It is also true that there is no more important part of a car than the engine, but it is not all the car is.

What is the mind?

This is a tricky question because it doesn't have a clear answer. The mind is a self-sufficient cognitive construct that we as a people still don't fully understand. Depending on who you are talking to and what their field of study is, you are liable to come up with many different definitions. One can go in a spiritual direction toward the answer, or one can go in a scientific way. You can fill up an entire library with the different ways people have attempted to answer that one question.

I will not even attempt to broach such a vast subject. Anything I say here will be a gross injustice to the true magnitude of what the Mind, rather, *Your Mind* actually is. My goal is to give some basic information as opposed to an in-depth synopsis.

I hope to lay some simple groundwork for you to begin the process of self-discovery and begin to see the vision of who you really can be. It should be enough to establish a basis for understanding.

Much ado has been made about the importance of appreciating the power of your mind (and for very, good reason). With that recognition has come some tremendous confusion as to how to tap into that power. Mankind has made some great strides in its attempts to grasp the power of the mind. But the concept of the mind is simply this: no matter how far, how wide, or how deep one goes, you can always go further, wider, and deeper.

The mind is the seat of consciousness, the essence of your being.

Paradigms, beliefs, personality, behavior, perceptions, attitudes, emotions (feelings), and relationships with yourself and others are all integrated to make up the mind. Your mind gives things meaning, and your meaning determines your motivation for actions.

A search on Wikipedia regarding the "Mind" states:

> It is generally agreed that the mind is that which enables a being to have subjective awareness and intentionality towards their environment, to perceive and respond to stimuli with some kind of agency, and to have consciousness, including thinking and feeling. Broadly speaking, mental faculties are the various functions of the mind, or things the mind can "do." Thought is a mental act that allows humans to make sense of things in the world, and to represent and interpret them in ways that are significant, or which accord with their needs, attachments, goals, commitments, plans, ends, desires, etc. Thinking involves the symbolic or semiotic mediation of ideas or data, as when we form concepts, engage in problem solving, reasoning, and making decisions. Words that refer to similar concepts and processes include deliberation, cognition, ideation, discourse and imagination. Thinking is sometimes described as a "higher" cognitive function and the analysis of thinking processes is a part of cognitive psychology. It is also deeply connected with our capacity to make and use tools; to understand cause and effect; to recognize patterns of significance; to comprehend and disclose unique contexts of experience or activity; and to respond to the world in a meaningful way.[22]

If there is any debate about the importance of your mind, the Bible says, "Let this mind be in you that was also in Christ Jesus." Philippians 2:5. This should end all debate as to how crucial having the right mindset is.

---

[22] Mind. Wikipedia. Last accessed 2018. https://en.wikipedia.org/wiki/Mind

MASTER YOUR MENTALITY

"And be not conformed to this world:
but be ye transformed by the renewing of your mind,
that ye may prove what is that good, and acceptable, and perfect, will of God."
— Romans 12:2

God commands us to renew our minds. Therefore, our mind must match that mandate. Why? Because you cannot live beyond your belief. I bring up belief here because you must understand the connection between what you believe and how you behave. According to Romans 12:2, God's desire is for you to renew your mind so that He can see His will carried out in your life. *You carry out His Will by how you live; you live by how you behave; and you behave by how you believe.*

Renewal of the mind is a process of *Being* that begins with believing and ends with behaving. This is paramount to note because right-believing leads to right-behaving, and right-behaving leads to right-believing.

Believing is a decision, not a feeling.

You change your mind by doing (James 4:7).

So, make the decision and then start doing. Remember, you change your Paradigm via Repetition— by taking (committed, consistent, and continual) action from where you are (Be) and working towards who you want to Become.

But it begins with belief.

"Jesus said unto him,
'If thou canst believe, all things are possible to him that believeth.'"
— Mark 9:23

The foundation of faith is belief. Belief begins where reason ends. Often, we want all the answers to have it fully figured out before we are willing to move forward. It just doesn't work like that. This brings us to the first component of MPOWER—Mastering your Mentality.

Mastering your mentality is connected to attitude and acceptance because there are some things that you just must accept. There is an old maxim that says, *"To those with faith, no explanation is necessary—to those without faith, no explanation will do."* Developing a positive, mental attitude must be accepted as truth and practiced if you have any hope of being successful.

These are the efforts it will take to master your mentality. The whole point is to fully embrace transformation; for growth in your mindset, in your attitude, in how you handle things better to be your way of life. Continuing with all your being to please God in all your actions, because you know if you do it, and you continue to learn so that you can be better in your talk as well as your walk.

Master your mentality to show your maturity. Growth in God means, *"being perfect even as your Father is perfect." (Matthew 5:48).*

MIND"SET"

"A mindset is quite literally a setting of the mind. It is a lens or frame of mind which orients an individual to a particular set of associations and expectations."
— **Dr. Alia Crum**

A Google search of "mindset" yields this definition: *the established set of attitudes held by someone.* Whenever you say mindset, people typically have an idea of what you are referring to. However, have you ever wondered why it is called mind**set**?

There are a couple of schools of thought here:

You have a mind that is set

Or

You have a set of minds

Truthfully, it is both.

Not only is it about setting your mind, but it is also about which mind you are setting.

When we don't see change, it could be for one of two reasons:

1. We haven't really set our minds on change. We go through the motions with no real commitment, and therein, we see no results.

2. We haven't set the right mind on change, meaning we consciously put forth the effort, but subconsciously we really don't believe we're going to see any results.

I said earlier that your "mindset matters." Now I simply want to add this: not only does your mindset matter, but also *which mind you set matters*.

Stanford University psychologist Carol S. Dweck, Ph.D., wrote in her book, *Mindset: The New Psychology of Success*, that there are essentially two mindsets that people can have: either a "fixed mindset" or a "growth mindset."[23]

She is referring to how a person's mind is actually *set* towards non-achievement/failure or growth/success.

❖ A *Fixed Mindset* comes from the belief that your qualities are carved in stone – who you are is who you are, period. Characteristics such

---

[23] Dweck, Carol. Mindset: The New Psychology of Success (New York City: Ballantine Books, a division of Penguin Random House LLC.; 2007); pages 6-9

as intelligence, personality, and creativity are fixed traits, rather than something that can be developed.

❖ A *Growth Mindset* comes from the belief that your basic qualities are things you can cultivate through effort. Yes, people differ greatly – in aptitude, talents, interests, or temperaments – but everyone can change and grow through application and experience.

The **fixed mindset** stands in the way of development and change. The **growth mindset** is a starting point for change, but people need to decide for themselves where their efforts toward change would be most valuable.

Having the right mindset will single-handedly determine whether you stay stuck or succeed.

$$E + R = O$$
(Event + Response = Outcome)

The above formula was popularized by Personal Development Guru Jack Canfield.[24] As the cliché goes, you are 10% of what happens to you and 90% of how you respond to it. The only thing you can control is your behavior (i.e. response). The problem is oftentimes we don't respond, we react, then that reaction yields an outcome we regret.

The MPOWER way of saying the same previous formula is:

$$C + C = C$$
(Circumstance + Choice = Consequence)

No matter what your circumstances are, you always have a choice, and it is your choice that can help determine the consequences. Bad circumstances do not automatically equal a bad consequences if you make a good choice. Keep

---

[24] Canfield, Jack. The Success Principles: How to get from Where You Are to Where You Want to Be (New York City: HarperCollins Publishers; 2015); pages 6-7

this in your heart: "I am shaped by my genetics, influenced by my circumstances, but defined by my choices."

Say this out loud: "I AM RESPONSIBLE FOR HOW I RESPOND TO SITUATIONS, EVEN THOSE I DIDN'T CREATE!"

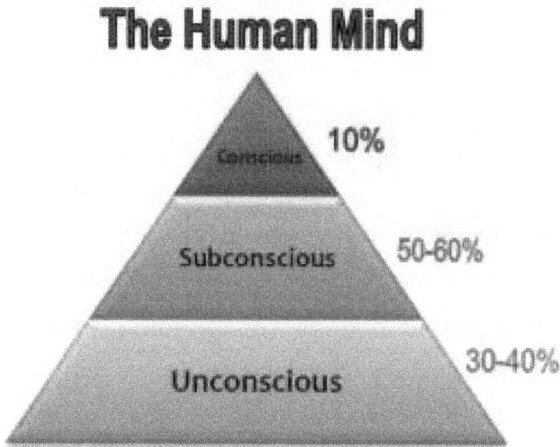

The Human Mind

Conscious 10%

Subconscious 50-60%

Unconscious 30-40%

I'm sure you heard of the theory of the "iceberg" as a means to describe the makeup of the mind. The iceberg is a wonderful analogy for obvious reasons. The tip of the iceberg is exposed yet way more of it is hidden under the sea. The part of your mind that represents the exposed part of the iceberg is your conscious mind with the rest of it meaning your subconscious and unconscious mind being what is not seen.

The mind is usually referred to as a whole, but actually exists in three distinctive parts[25] (as noted in the diagram above):

❖ The Conscious Mind is where your intellect, perspective, and awareness reside.

---

[25] A Walk Through the Human Mind. Last accessed 2018.
http://www.ascend25d.com/index.php/2016/04/27/a-walk-through-the-human-mind/

❖ The Subconscious Mind is where your intuition, paradigms, and attitudes reside.

❖ The Unconscious Mind is where your instincts, phobias, and auto-activity (i.e., breathing, heartbeat, etc.) reside.

For this discussion, I want to focus on the subconscious mind. To see success, it is the subconscious mind that has to make the shifts. When it comes to elevating the mind (i.e. thinking on another level), you have to do it subconsciously.

The Subconscious Mind responds to... "See it, Say it, Seize it!"

See It

Clarity: In the form of Actualization.

Actualization begins with visualization. To actualize a thing is to make it real, in your mind's eye first. Create a mental picture with vivid details of your preferred life. The more detailed, the better. You must become crystal clear about where you want to be in life. However, this does not always mean the path to get you there will be crystal clear. You may not even see a path at all. But this is not the time to be worried about "how" you will get there. This will be worked out soon enough. We will dig deeper into "Creating Clarity," in Chapter 9. For now, just know that your world will be a reflection of the mirror of your mind. The clearer the picture is, the more real it will become; literally.

You Become what you Behold.

Andrew Carnegie, the mentor of Napoleon Hill, once said, *"Any idea that is held in the mind, that is emphasized, that is either feared or revered, will begin at once to cloth itself in the most convenient and appropriate form available."*

In other words, the basic operating principle of consciousness is that any thought, plan, goal, or idea held continuously (via visualization) in the subconscious mind must be brought into reality.

P.S.

- This works for both positive and negative thoughts.

Say It

Commands: In the form of Affirmations

Your subconscious mind will obey whatever you say. The key is "repeatedly." Paint the picture in your mind's eye with words. Say what you see, so you can see what you say. But say it with feeling, so you can feel what you are saying. Just don't be wishy washy (James 1:5-8).

Food for thought: the subconscious mind does not respond to words like can't, don't, won't, etc. The mind will drop or not recognize the negative participle "not." For example, consciously, you say, "*don't* slam the door;" subconsciously, you hear "*do* slam the door," inadvertently, the door gets slammed. Therefore, say what you *will do* to create your new normal, not what you *won't do*. Say "I *will* exercise three times a week and eat healthier." Not, "I *won't* lie around on the couch eating chips." (You will have to be more specific than that in your affirmations, but I think you get the point.) Look in the mirror and speak with authority, with specificity, and with finality to your reality.

Seize It

Commitment: In the form of Activation

Your reality won't change until your behavior does. Your words mean nothing if you don't follow through with committed action. I use the word "committed" here because you will not achieve the results you desire with "temporary" change. The only way to create a new reality is to slay the bad habits that created your current reality. Your actions must align with your picture of your desired destination.

SUBLIMINAL SUGGESTION

"Thought attracts that upon which it is directed."
— **Claude M. Bristol**

There are many subtle suggestions that we make to ourselves that are either harmful or helpful. Have you ever considered the things suggested to you subliminally? This type of messaging is all around us and in us, trying to influence us one way or the other. The right subliminal suggestion supports our success. The wrong subliminal suggestion sabotages us subconsciously.

"For the thing which I greatly feared is come upon me,
and that which I was afraid of is come unto me."
— **Job 3:25**

The above scripture is a wonderful example of what Andrew Carnegie meant by the word "feared" (mentioned earlier). We see Job, who had a fear (a negative thought) and put so much energy into trying to prevent it that it came into reality. You must be careful about the subliminal suggestions (either externally or internally) that you allow to get embedded in your subconscious mind because they will bring forth results.

PUT YOUR HEART AND SOUL INTO IT

I would be remiss if I did not mention that the Bible uses heart, soul, and mind interchangeably at times.

"And thou shalt love Lord thy God with all thy heart,
and with all thy soul, and with all thy mind,
and with all thy strength: this is the first commandment."
— **Mark 12:30**

❖ The Heart is considered the center of a person's being. Essentially, your core. That's why you hear clichés like *"let's get to the heart of the matter."*

❖ Your Soul is made up of your will, intellect, and emotion.

❖ The Mind is where your different levels of consciousness reside.

Although they may have different names and different definitions – in the original Hebrew and Greek, they still are so synonymous they are essentially the same.

"Beloved, I wish above all things that thou mayest prosper and be in health, even as thy soul prospereth."
— 3 John 2

The Greek word here for soul is *psyche,* which is defined in the Merriam-Webster dictionary as *the totality of elements forming the mind.* This denotes to me that your heart and your soul go together to form what we know today as the mind.

"For as he thinketh in his heart, so is he."
— Proverbs 23:7

The word heart here is literally translated as the *activity of the mind.*

"But when Jesus perceived their thoughts, He answering said unto them, What reason ye in your hearts?"
— Luke 5:22

The Greek word here for heart is "Kardia." It means *the middle or central or inmost part of anything, the soul or mind, as it is the fountain and seat of the thoughts, passions, desires, appetites, affections, purposes, endeavors, and emotions.*

My goal in pointing out these three individual yet connected components was to help you understand scripturally how complex the human mind's make-up is.

PERSONAL EXCELLENCE

Excellence means *possessing outstanding quality or superior merit; being so to an extreme degree; of the highest or finest quality; exceptionally good for its kind.*

*"Forasmuch as an **excellent spirit**, and knowledge, and understanding, interpreting of dreams, and shewing of hard sentences, and dissolving of doubts, were found in the same Daniel."*
— **Daniel 5:12**

*"Then this Daniel was preferred above the presidents and princes, because an **excellent spirit** was in him; and the king thought to set him over the whole realm."*
— **Daniel 6:3**

To have an excellent spirit means that while you may not have the resources of the other person, you don't make excuses as to why what you produce is not the best that you can do with what you do have at your disposal. Excellence is a definite standard to which you hold yourself to. It is your ability to do a thing to the highest order to which you can do it. Excellence is you doing the very best with what you have to work with.

The only real competition is yourself, because truthfully, only you can stop you. I define excellence as *bettering your best.* Tell yourself, "Until my best is better, **I will always be the better me.**" When you think you have done it to the best that you can do, at that point, do it better. That is excellence.

The moment you think you can't do something is the moment you can't do it (Philippians 4:13). You are who and what you think you are. Your reality is determined by your mentality. Think better and you will be better, but think great and you will be great (Proverbs 23:7a).

Personal excellence means a continuous improvement of self. It is embracing the challenge to master your mindset.

SEE YOURSELF AS A SUCCESS

This entire chapter was designed to do one thing: to get you to see yourself as a success. The whole idea behind elevating your mind and mastering your mentality is so that you could not only see beyond where you are, but you see yourself beyond where you are. You don't just see greater potential; you see your newly realized life.

You must expose yourself to something greater than yourself. Here is how you begin this process of exposure:

Create visuals for yourself. Do a vision board of pictures of your ideal life: the type of house you want to live in, the type of car(s) you want to drive, the type of vacations you want to take, the type of career/ business you want to have, etc. Listen to things that will expand your horizons, things that will help you be a better you. Speak with people who are more successful than you. You would be amazed at how willing successful people are to have a conversation that will be a blessing to you.

The second part of the process of exposure is to change your experiences. Go to an expensive restaurant, if you can. Then get what you want without worrying about the price. If that's not possible right now, just get water and an appetizer or salad. Go to a five-star hotel and get a room. If you can't, then sit in the lobby to write your thoughts and ideas. Go to luxury car dealerships and take test drives. If you can't do that, looking around is free. Drive through neighborhoods with luxury homes, and go to open houses where possible.

Put yourself in situations to have a different experience that is better than where you are. Exposure creates expectation. Once you see it, you can be it. Simply reverse engineer what you see, create a plan, and go after it.

IF YOU REALLY WANT TO SUCCEED
THEN
SEE YOURSELF AS A SUCCESS

MPOWER ME

CHAPTER 7

Master Your Methodology

*"Formal Education will make you a living,
while Self-Education will make you a fortune."*
— **Jim Rohn**

EDUCATE YOURSELF ON METHODS

We struggle with *"HOW."* Whenever there is something that needs to get done, typically *How* is the biggest question that we face, and yet it is also the easiest one to answer. I find it interesting because it is not a question of why I should do it, nor of what I should do.

But, often it is "how do I do it"?

But that is always a question you can answer in your current situation.

You just need to *Elevate Your Mind.*

Using the *Law of Perspective* from an elevated consciousness gives you the ability to see solutions where you once only saw problems. From there, *Educate Yourself on Methods*

*"And he shall be like a tree planted by the rivers of water, that bringeth forth his fruit in his season; his leaf also shall not wither; and **whatsoever** he doeth shall prosper."*
— **Psalm 1:3 (emphasis added)**

The word *"Whatsoever"* is a huge indicator as to what God thinks of *"HOW."* You must understand that the *Methodology* is your responsibility.

The major difference between what to do and how to do it in one word is "details."

If you notice, God doesn't always specialize in the specifics, He gives broad instructions like: "leave your country and go to a land that I will show thee." (Genesis 12:1)

The specifics of how you do what He tells you to do most of the time are always up to you.

Just DO it.

You're probably still saying, "Yeah, but I don't know what to do."

> *"Sometimes you have to jump*
> *and figure out how to fly.*
> *Everything is 'figure out' able."*
> **— Nick F. Nelson**
> *(The "Brandpreneur")*

Beloved, let me say this as kindly as possible—*FIGURE IT OUT!*

Whenever we find ourselves not able to move forward, this is because of something we don't know. Biblically put, *"my people perish for lack of knowledge" (Hosea 4:6)*. Whenever God desires for you to do something, the question then becomes how? You must ask yourself, "How can I learn what it is that He wants me to do?" This is why I call this **Self-Education** (which I will go through in greater detail in a moment).

MASTER YOUR METHODOLOGY

Your methodology reveals your mindset. This is why there is a need for self-education because there are no significant accomplishments if your ability does not match your mentality.

Educate yourself on methods. What does that mean exactly? In a nutshell, it is *gathering all pertinent information and "know-how" necessary for you to succeed in your area of proficiency.* As the second component of MPOWER, this connects with the accuracy of your aptitude as you cultivate your professional expertise.

Mastery of your methodology is about equipping yourself with the tools and knowing the tactics to excel in your chosen arena. This could mean pursuing traditional education, getting a certain certification for credibility, or having a conversation with a mentor or peer to figure out what worked for them and what could potentially work for you.

This is self-education. What do you need to know to succeed that will tap into your gift and increase your professionalism and value? In other words, when you learn more, you earn more.

You must hone your skills. The main word I want to point out is the word "your." Take ownership of what God gave you! The goal is to turn your passion and your purpose into your profession. Don't just go to school and get a degree in anything, don't just get a job doing anything, but position yourself to take advantage of what comes to you naturally and get paid for it. This is the shift that you need to make to master the methods of your strengths.

Do you have the Training (i.e., know the procedures), do you know the Terminology (i.e., know the policies), and what are the Techniques (i.e., know the practices) to accomplish the tasks for a career in this field?

When you know more, you grow more. As the saying goes, "If you knew better, you'd do better." The whole goal of self-education is learning to do what needs to be done effectively and efficiently to accomplish your objectives.

Ever heard the cliché, "Don't be a one-trick pony?" My use here implies having more in your bag of tricks than just your "talent." It is about training as much as it is about talent, because talent alone is never enough.

I do not want you to be confused by that last sentence, as though I am backpedaling on what I said earlier about the importance of *Talent*. I am saying here that talent must be cultivated in order to be maximized.

> *"And beside this, giving all diligence, add to your faith virtue; and to virtue knowledge; And to knowledge temperance; and to temperance patience; and to patience godliness; And to godliness brotherly kindness; and to brotherly kindness charity. For if these things be in you, and abound, they make you that ye shall neither be barren nor unfruitful in the knowledge of our Lord Jesus Christ."*
> **— 2 Peter 1:5-8**

Add to your arsenal and multiply your means:

Grow "**YOU**," then grow what you do.

GIVE YOUR GIFT

> *"Your real strength comes from being the best 'YOU' you can be.*
> *So who are you? What are you good at? What do you love?*
> *What makes you, 'YOU'?"*
> **— "PO"**
> *(Kung Fu Panda 3)*

Unfortunately, we as individuals tend to maximize the greatness of others and minimize our own. Oftentimes, we discount what is unique about ourselves, when our uniqueness is what makes us great.

Unique is defined as *being the only one of its kind, unlike anything else.* You fall into that category. Your uniqueness is God's gift to you; how you utilize your uniqueness is your gift to Him.

> *"As each one has received a special gift, employ it in serving one another as good stewards of the manifold grace of God."*
> **— 1 Peter 4:10 (NASB)**

> *"A man's gift maketh room for him, and bringeth him before great men."*
> **— Proverbs 18:16**

In Chapter 2, we mentioned the Parable of the Talents (Matthew 25:14-30). All three servants were given at least one talent. We love to get caught up in the quantity, but it is about the quality. The servant with five talents was no better than the servant with one talent. The reward was equal based on how they used it. The servant with two talents received the same as the servant with five talents. And had the servant with one talent used what he had, he too would have been told, "Well done." Instead, he hid the talent that he had and was considered wicked as a result of not using the special gift he was given.

Is that you?

Remember earlier when I said, "The wealth of the sinner is laid up for the just?" I established the case that it is the same person. It is all about being in or out of God's will. Because the servant with one talent hid what he had, not only was the talent taken away, but he was also referred to as a wicked servant. I said sinner/wicked is another way of saying outside of the will of God.

The only guideline that God requires is for you to take advantage of your gifting, your skill set, and your ability. That's where accuracy comes in as the second part of getting the lock to open. Accurately utilizing your aptitude is the only way that you can tap into true prosperity.

Remember this definition of Aptitude:

> *Your God given ability to fulfill your purpose by using your learned skills, natural talents, and spiritual gifts.*

Then I said:

BECAUSE YOU HAVE NOT ACCURATELY UTILIZED YOUR APTITUDE, THAT IS WHY YOU ARE NOT SUCCESSFUL!

Think of the people on Earth who are the wealthiest and most successful (e.g., entrepreneurs, celebrities, professional athletes, movie stars, etc.). They typically are those who are using their talent or gift in some shape, form, or fashion.

Don't hide the Gift God gave you. Use it to His glory.

FACULTIES OF THE MIND

I could have mentioned these *"Faculties of the Mind"* in the last chapter, but I saved them, because I believe they're more fitting here.

Most people think their only connection to the material world is through their 5 Senses:

- Sound, Sight, Smell, Taste, and Touch.

Nothing could be further from the truth. We also have higher faculties of the mind which deepen the connection to our environment. That is why being in the right place *(Law of Place)* is critically important, so even if you can't be there physically you can be there mentally.

Faculties are defined as:

1. Exceptional ability, natural or acquired, for a particular kind of action; aptitude
2. One of the powers of the mind
3. An inherent capability of the body

"An educated person is a person who has so developed the faculties of their mind that they can acquire anything they want or its equivalent without violating the rights of others."
— Napoleon Hill

You have six higher faculties of the mind. Knowing these higher faculties and how they work is part of the developmental process for *Mastering your Methodology.*

Reason

The faculty of reason is your capacity for consciously making sense of things, establishing and verifying facts, applying logic, and changing or justifying practices, institutions, and beliefs based on new or existing information.

Memory

The faculty of memory is the mental capacity of retaining and reviving facts, events, impressions, information, etc., or of recalling or recognizing previous experiences. Your memory faculty connects you to the past, present, and future.

Perception

The faculty of perception is most commonly known as our point of view. But it can be more aptly defined as our recognition and interpretation of sensory information. Perception also includes how we respond to the information. We can think of perception as a process where we take in sensory information from our environment and use that information to interact with our environment. Perception allows us to take the sensory information in and make it into something meaningful.

Will

The faculty of will is best defined as a process by which an individual decides on and commits to a particular course of action. Development of a strong will creates cognitive control, which allows you to be disciplined and deliberate to get goals accomplished.

Intuition

The faculty of intuition has been described as a sixth sense, a gut feeling, a hunch, or the infamous "something told me..." The truth is the intuition is a mental factor, the inborn capacity of the human mind for acquiring entirely new information, knowledge and understanding without the use of one's familiar faculties of reasoning, sensing and memory. We can define intuition as an instant idea or an immediate answer we receive without even thinking about it.

Imagination

The easiest way to define imagination is to repeat the words of Bob Proctor because he put it best when he said, "The imagination is that mental faculty that gives us the ability to tap into the "no" thing (i.e. nothing) and bring into our consciousness a magnificent image that we can use to transform our life."

EMOTIONAL INTELLIGENCE

"Decades of research point to emotional intelligence,
as the critical factor that sets star performers apart from the rest of the pack."
— Travis Bradberry

I wanted to mention emotional intelligence here because it is not something we hear a lot about, but it is extremely important. Truthfully, studies have shown that a leader's emotional intelligence (EI) is a far more effective indicator for success than his/her intelligence quotient (IQ).

Stated simply, being smart is good, but being stable and steady makes you better.

Adapted from the Article: Why You Need Emotional Intelligence to Succeed.[26] By Travis Bradberry

Your emotional intelligence is the foundation for a host of critical skills—and it impacts most everything you do and say.

How much of an impact does emotional intelligence have on your professional success? The short answer is: a lot! It's a powerful way to focus your energy in one direction with a tremendous result.

Emotional intelligence is the "something" in each of us that is a bit intangible. It affects how we manage behavior, navigate social complexities, and make personal decisions that achieve positive results.

Emotional intelligence is made up of four core skills that pair up under two primary competencies: personal competence and social competence.

Personal competence comprises your self-awareness and self-management skills, which focus more on you individually than on your interactions with other people. Personal competence is your ability to stay aware of your emotions and manage your behavior and tendencies.

❖ Self-awareness is your ability to accurately perceive your emotions and stay aware of them as they happen.

---

[26] Bradberry, Travis. Why You Need Emotional Intelligence to Succeed. January 25, 2016: www.success.com/article/why-you-need-emotional-intelligence-to-succeed

❖ Self-management is your ability to use awareness of your emotions to stay flexible and positively direct your behavior.

Social competence is made up of your social awareness and relationship management skills; social competence is your ability to understand other people's moods, behavior and motives in order to respond effectively and improve the quality of your relationships.

❖ Social awareness is your ability to accurately pick up on emotions in other people and understand what is really going on.

❖ Relationship management is your ability to use awareness of your emotions and the others' emotions to manage interactions successfully.

Emotional intelligence taps into a fundamental element of human behavior that is distinct from your intellect. There is no known connection between IQ and emotional intelligence; you simply can't predict emotional intelligence based on how smart someone is. Intelligence is your ability to learn, and it's the same at age fifteen as it is at age fifty. Emotional intelligence, on the other hand, is a flexible set of skills that can be acquired and improved with practice. Although some people are naturally more emotionally intelligent than others, you can develop high emotional intelligence even if you aren't born with it.

DO IT WITH DIGNITY

To say *"do it with dignity"* is the same thing as saying *"do it with 'Class.'"*

No matter where you currently find yourself, or what *Season of Life* you're in, the work you are doing means something.

Dignity is a sense of pride in oneself, self-respect. The state or quality of being worthy of honor.

Dignity is what separates the real from the fake. It lends credibility to your character and your career. It ensures that you have legitimacy and respect in the marketplace. Whatever you do in life or in business, do it with dignity. Dignity requires discipline and proves whether you are serious about your success.

Dignity and excellence complement each other. They are different sides of the same coin. You can't do stuff in excellence without doing it with dignity, and you can't do stuff with dignity without doing it with excellence.

This is important because the dignity with which you go about doing your work, shows your appreciation for the work you do. That authentic appreciation is always rewarded, no matter what the work is.

STUDY YOUR WAY TO SUCCESS

If there is a *K.E.Y* to success in life, it is to…

Keep
Educating
Yourself

Lifelong learning is the voluntary and self-motivated pursuit of knowledge for either personal or professional reasons. It is the learners, those willing to open their minds and continually add to their skillsets, who will be poised to succeed in the future. Know what you need to know, so you can grow where you need to grow, and go where you need to go.

> *Wisdom is the principal thing; therefore, get wisdom: and with all thy getting get understanding. Proverbs 4:7*

IF YOU REALLY WANT TO SUCCEED
THEN
STUDY YOUR WAY TO SUCCESS

MPOWER ME

CHAPTER 8

Master Your Modality

"Success is a result of implementation, not contemplation."
— **Roger Daye**

"Good habits don't just happen, but Bad habits do."
— **Anonymous**

EVALUATE YOUR MODEL

The MPOWER Philosophy is three-fold:

1. Elevate your Mind
2. Educate yourself on Methods
3. Evaluate your Model

Evaluate means to assess, adjust, and accomplish.

- ❖ Assess – Calculate the Course
- ❖ Adjust – Correct the Course (when/where necessary)
- ❖ Accomplish – Complete the Course

Model: a system or thing used as an example to follow or imitate.

What do I mean when I say, "Evaluate your model"?

You must understand that everything you do in life has been modeled for you at some point. Whether that is something or someone close to you or something or someone that you have seen from afar, you are following a model.

Is it burdensome or beneficial? Is it a blessing that you do things that way, or are they some bad habits that you picked up along the way? Evaluate your Model!

The actions you do take and even the actions you don't take come from a certain model.

Therefore, we say to evaluate that model.

If you are not successful to the degree that you can be, it can only come from the model that you are using.

From the Fortune 500 company to the individual employee, anything or anyone making money is using a business model. The Fortune 500 company put together a business plan, acquired start-up capital, and went into business. The employee filled out an application, was offered the job, and went to work. Both make money, but how they make it is vastly different. Anything that we do at some point was modeled for us. The question is, what model are you using?

Dean Graziosi once said, "The fastest way to your next level is learning from those who are already doing it."

I ask you two questions: who are you imitating that you need to stop, and who are you not imitating that you need to start?

Modeling is allowing yourself to be influenced by people who are where you want to be and simply doing what they did to get there.

Let me be clear: this is not about you becoming a copycat, rather it is you acknowledging what worked for them and seeing if it will work for you while staying true to who you are.

You are looking for philosophy, perspective, principles, patterns, and practices to see what you can implement in your life.

Remember, the "Combination to Success" is Attitude, Aptitude, and Action.

The "Action" part of the combination comes into play in this last part of the MPOWER Philosophy. Evaluate your model because it is all about *what* you are doing.

"To live through an impossible situation, you don't need the reflexes of a grand prix driver or the strength of a Hercules or the mind of an Einstein. You simply need to know what to do."
— Anthony Greenbank

Modality, by definition, is *an attribute or circumstance that denotes mode or manner.* It is a breakdown of a person's mode, which means a way of doing something, expressing something, or acting. The MPOWER definition of modality is *the way you get things done.* At MPOWER, modality is literally the actions you take for accomplishment.

This outlines the last part of the Combination to Success—**"YOUR"** ACTIONS.

PROFITABLE EXECUTION

The idea here is for "Profitable Execution," which certainly is not to be confused with perfect execution (which is only necessary in brain surgery).

As long as you are not performing brain surgery, you do not need to be perfect. But if you and your business are to be successful, you must focus on Profitability.

As Wallace Wattles says in his book, The Science of Getting Rich, "An individual can get rich by doing certain things in a certain way."[27] This is the same way you must become profitable—you must do certain things in a certain way.

The MPOWER approach ascribes this particular way of doing things as Profitable Execution.

Most people believe execution is mastering the art of getting things done. Conversely, it is *a discipline,* so much more than just getting things done.

This *"Execution"* is what I call the "Discipline of Doing."

It is not just doing stuff to be doing stuff. This is what is left out in society's current understanding of Execution and why it is not just about *getting things done.* It is all about getting the *right* things done.

Back to the example of the Fortune 500 company and the employee (mentioned in Chapter 3)— what is different? One trades products or services for profit, whereas the other trades time for dollars. Do you see the profound difference? You can always make more products to make more profit, but you can't make more time to make more dollars.

Here is a caveat I want you to think about: In the eyes of the IRS both are considered businesses. One has an EIN (or Employer Identification Number), the other has an SSN (or Social Security Number). Each denotes the way they create income and how they can be taxed. All I'm saying is, if you are going to be treated like a business, you need to start acting like a business.

It needs to become *YOU, Inc.*

Evaluate the model that you have been using to make money, and utilize a model that is more successful.

---

[27] Wattles, Wallace. The Science of Getting Rich, Abridged Edition. (Pennsylvania: Tremendous Life Books); page 11

Here is how you incorporate the Fortune 500 business model into your life: the products they trade for profit are not always tangible. Sometimes those products are more about creating something of value that can be monetized, for which people are willing to pay.

From real estate (tangible product) to coaching and consulting (intangible product), how can you use your gift to create value and become more profitable?

You must *produce* something of value in order to *profit*.

I want you to Elevate your Mindset so that you understand that the money you bring in, whether it is from a paycheck (as an employee) or payments (as an entrepreneur), is all considered profit.

Then Educate yourself on Methods to understand, profits can be increased; you just need to figure out how to increase them in your life.

Lastly, Evaluate your Model, to take the actions conducive to creating that kind of growth for yourself.

Think broadly about your options. Get creative, because change is possible for you.

If others have come from worse conditions than you and were able to turn their situations around, then what is your excuse? What did they do that you have not? Everything is "figure-out-able."

It is execution versus excuses. If business is bad, then blame the CEO you see in the mirror. You are the Chief Executive Officer of your life (remember, it is YOU, Inc.)

> *"You should never wish for something you are not willing to work for.*
> *Your expectations cannot exceed your efforts."*
> **— Inky Johnson**

SUCCESSFUL BUSINESS MODEL

Every successful business has a model, and some of these models can be quite complex. The simplest way to break them down is to find the common denominators.

The three staples of any good business are:

1. Structure
2. Strategy
3. System

Any and every successful business has these three things in common, although they may have different ways of implementing and executing them.

Structure

Structure is the way a thing is constructed, built, arranged, or organized. There are Legal Structures, Management Structures, Organizational Structures, etc. In business, the structure creates stability. What you want to take from this is the fact that you need a structure of success for your life.

Strategy

A plan of action or policy designed to achieve a major or overall aim. Problems arise when we don't stick to the strategy. Plan your work, then work your plan.

What is your P.L.A.N.?

- ❖ Prioritized – What's Important Now (W.I.N.)?
- ❖ List – How will you carry this out?
- ❖ Actions – What steps must you take?
- ❖ Needed – Keep the main thing the main thing.

The purpose of a plan is to give yourself a means to stay on task and on track.

System

A system is a specific series of steps to achieve success. Systematization leads to monetization because it creates scalability.

A good S.Y.S.T.E.M. *S*aves, *Y*ou, *S*tress, *T*ime, *E*nergy, and *M*oney.

Your System must be:

1. Simple (easily understood).
2. Step-by-Step (easily duplicated).
3. Successful (easily produces results).

THE DISCIPLINE OF DOING

"History does not record those people who did nothing,
history only records those people who did something."
— Anonymous

It was 4 (something) *a.m.* and I kept hitting the snooze button on the alarm clock. I felt as though I just needed a little more sleep. My dilemma? I had recently committed to the sacrifice of getting up earlier to finish this book. Therefore, I made the decision that every day I would get up at 4:00 A.M. precisely to work on it. Well, that didn't go as planned. When it came time to get up, I felt so tired that I thought, *Just a little more sleep, then I will get up.* However, I'm sure you have felt this same feeling, and the issue was that I felt like I couldn't really get back to sleep. That fifteen-minute snooze button felt like fifteen seconds. This wasting of time went on until I heard these words in my spirit,

"Good Intentions Are Always Outweighed By Poor Actions"

In other words, what you DO will always matter more than what you say!

"Lazy people want much but get little, but those who work hard will prosper."
— Proverbs 13:4 (NLT)

To succeed, you must develop a "Discipline of Doing" and you must do it now! Will Smith once said, "Self-discipline is at the center of material wealth."

There are three defining characteristics of a person with Discipline:

- ❖ Determination – the willingness to do what it takes to succeed.
- ❖ Dedication – seeing a thing through until completion.
- ❖ Dependability – the trust factor that lets people know they can count on you.

What is wonderful is that discipline and these three characteristics that accompany it are not exclusive to select, special human beings, but rather, they can be cultivated by anyone willing to make the commitment and do the work. An individual must go from imagination to implementation.

"I have a short bridge between the thinking land and the doing land,
whereas a lot of people have a long bridge."
— Raymond Aaron

You need to execute like your life depends on it, because it does, or at least your *quality of life*. You live the life you are designed and destined to live depends upon what you do.

Here is your recipe for the Discipline of Doing:

- ❖ Model: find the best example of execution for what you want to accomplish.

- ❖ Modify: Whatever you model, you must make your own. Remember that the Combination to Success requires you to *accurately use your aptitude*.

❖ Move: The point is *progress*. Focus Forward by Going God-ward.

DO IT NOW

When do you take advantage of the opportunity you have been given?

You must take advantage of an opportunity of a lifetime in the lifetime of the opportunity. You don't have forever to be great.

N.O.W. is an acronym that stands for *No Opportunity Wasted*. You do not want to look back on your past and see a life full of regrets where you did not take advantage of ALL that was presented to you time after time. If you are clothed in your right mind and have life, health, and strength, then every day you wake up, you have been given an opportunity.

Anything God desires for you to do, He wants you to do it NOW! This is a truth that you must embrace. There is a reason that the Bible says, "Now faith…" (in Hebrews 11:1). It is an emphatic expression that denotes priority. When do you want to activate the faith necessary to carry out God's will for your life? Later? Of course not. You certainly want to get started now. There has to be a sense of urgency that creates a motivation to win.

Jim Harbaugh (NFL Head Coach) said, "In order to W.I.N., you have to ask this question: What's important now?"

The reason you want to get started now is because there is always something important to do now; there is no time to waste, when it comes to the pursuit of your destiny.

DAILY DECISIONS DICTATE DESTINY

"Success does not come in a day, but success comes daily."
—Bishop Dale Bronner
(Senior Pastor at Word of Faith Cathedral)

I briefly mention this in the preface, but I'd like to go one step further on how to develop the discipline of getting things down through daily decisions. Brian Tracy put it best when he said, "Only through completion of daily tasks, can one see success."

Daily decisions dictate destiny. A good book that I would recommend on this subject is *The Slight Edge* by Jeff Olson. In this book, he says, "The truth is, what you do matters. What you do today matters. What you do every day matters."[28]

Learn from yesterday to do today what is best for tomorrow. Studies show that small, incremental actions taken consistently are much more effective at bringing about change and transformation. You should have some C.O.R.E. things you do daily:

*Consistent **O**rganized **R**outine **E**very day*

Most successful people have a morning ritual. This could include exercise, studying scripture and prayer, reading a book, or morning meditation. Not an exhaustive list, C.O.R.E. requires some sort of time for intentional effort to start the day on the right track. You cannot just wake up and see what happens that day. Dr. Cindy Trimm says, "Command your Morning."

> *"Either you run the day, or the day runs you."*
> **— Jim Rohn**

You must take control of your day and not let the day control you. Taking control of your day does not mean unexpected things won't happen. But I guarantee you by being prepared to the best of your ability to have a successful day by controlling the things you can, you will be much better equipped to deal with the things you can't control.

---

[28] Olsen, Jeff. The Slight Edge: Turning Simple Disciplines into Massive Success and Happiness (Austin: Greenleaf Book Group Press; 2013); page 58

I like Grant Cardone's approach in his book, *The 10X Rule*, where he says, "Everything is your fault, therefore, take responsibility for everything." He goes on to give this example: "Let's say you get into a car wreck this morning (God forbid), no matter who's at fault, it's your fault. People call car wrecks 'accidents,' but it is no accident. Somebody was somewhere they were not supposed to be. Because you can't control the other person, you are the one at fault. Because if you had gotten up earlier, planned and prepared your day, then left earlier for your appointment, you would not have been there at that time to be in that wreck, therefore it is your fault. Take responsibility for your day."[29]

That is an extreme example, but I think you get the point. Don't just be aloof, lethargic, indifferent, or *laissez-faire*, about your day, but command your morning! *DAILY* Decisions Dictate Destiny. Dominate your Day!

The Daily Action(s) you take should be:

- ❖ Powerful - you do it to the absolute best of your ability. Operate in Excellence.

- ❖ Proactive - a planned and practical action. You do what you CAN do, because Proactivity decreases Reactivity.

- ❖ Perpetual - your next action should build on the last action.

- ❖ Persistent - perseverance mixed with preparation.

You can download a free gift of a Powerful Prayer and a Daily Declaration at **www.mpower-me.info** to help get your day started with intention.

---

[29] Cardone, Grant. The 10X Rule: The Only Difference Between Success and Failure (Hoboken: John Wiley & Sons, Inc.; 2013); pages 40-43

FOUR REASONS PEOPLE DON'T SUCCEED

Because they are unwilling...

1. Excuses – Unwillingness to release ridiculous reasoning.
2. Effort – Unwillingness to do the necessary work.
3. Education – Unwillingness to learn a different/better way of doing things.
4. Execution – Unwillingness to fully commit to carry out the plan.

THREE REASONS WHY THINGS FAIL

Through a Lack of...

1. Relationships and Connections

Sometimes it is not only about who you know, but also who knows you. Leverage (via networking, both who you know and who you don't) and duplication (more of you through other people doing what you do) are the two ways to build your business with an entrepreneurial mindset.

2. Research and Choices

Ignorance is not bliss, because what you don't know can hurt you. Put the work in to find out what you need to succeed. Secondly, what you do (or don't do) with what you know can be an issue as well.

3. Resources and Capital

You must be a good steward of what God places in your hands. Know the difference between a seed and a harvest. God will always provide seed to the sower. That means He will give you seed to invest. The return on your investment (ROI) is the harvest. Here is where wisdom is critical: the greater the seed sown, the greater the harvest reaped. So, from that first seed that you sowed to when the harvest comes in, is it really another seed? Knowing the difference is the difference between success and failure.

WHAT IS YOUR GOAL?

Goals are one of those things in life that are necessary for success. It really is just that cut and dry. If you are not setting goals, then you are not serious about succeeding. If I must convince you of the importance of setting goals, then I'm not sure you're ready for this conversation about success. Because those who are truly ready to succeed understand the importance of goal setting. In these next few sections, I simply want to delve into some aspects of goal setting that you may not know, to help you get to where you are supposed to be. This is literally the purpose of a goal—to create a destination and give you a target for which to shoot.

Imagine someone wanting to go on a trip somewhere, yet they don't know how to get there, nor do they put the address in the GPS. They simply start driving! Now that is the equivalent of not setting a goal. If your efforts are like the bullets of a gun, then not setting goals is the equivalent of firing aimlessly into nothingness. You are wasting your bullets or efforts because you have no target to hit.

THREE PARTS TO A GOAL

BIG Beginning

Our initial efforts have the best of intentions at the beginning. We start strong.

Messy Middle

The gap between goal setting and goal achieving is sometimes greater than we anticipated. Especially when life hits or something unexpected happens. In the middle sometimes, things can get messy.

Expected End

This does not mean what you may think. It doesn't mean you get at the end what you expected at the beginning. It means, what did you expect you were going to get from the work you put in?

My aim is simply to make two, small tweaks in your mind (both consciously and subconsciously) about goal setting.

1. Are you setting SMART Goals?

   - **Specific**
   - **Measurable**
   - **Attainable**
   - **Relevant**
   - **Timeframe**

2. Shift your mind from goal setting to goal achieving. In your mind, do not say this is the goal I'm setting (because setting the goal should be automatic), make *achieving the goal* your focus. From this point on, as you are writing your goals say, "These are the goals I will achieve."

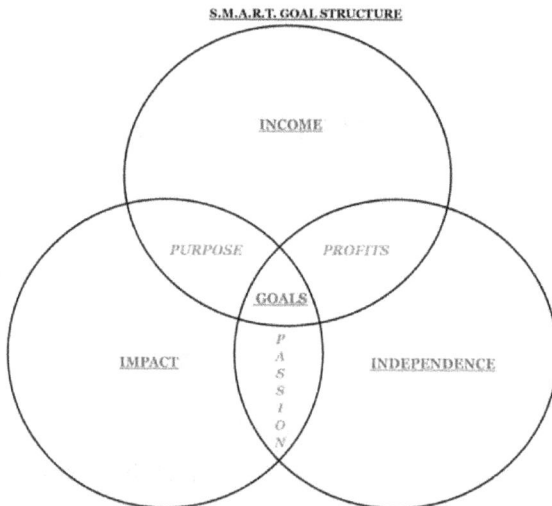

S.M.A.R.T. GOAL STRUCTURE

INCOME

PURPOSE   PROFITS

GOALS

IMPACT   INDEPENDENCE

P
A
S
S
I
O
N

The diagram shows the areas where you want to set your goals, with the sweet spot being all areas combined to make your major SMART goal. The three main areas are Income, Impact, and Independence.

1. Income is your finances. What is your fiscal responsibility?
2. Impact is where you focus your faith.
3. Independence is family, fun, and freedom.

Then interconnected are the deeper parts of your life being purpose, profits, and passion.

❖ Purpose is always going to be tied to your gifting and your calling, so you must utilize them to have an impact and see income from it. You want to be paid to do what you were built to do.

❖ Profits come from your income and independence because the money you make creates your quality of life.

❖ Passion is a mixture of your impact and your independence, meaning you have the freedom to give and serve towards your worthy cause.

You start out by setting a SMART goal in each individual area, then once you have those SMART goals set, you combine those smaller SMART goals to create one major SMART goal.

SMART GOAL For example:

> *Within the next five years, MPOWER will be a global phenomenon where people are taking advantage of the principles of this philosophy and their lives are changed for the better. From this endeavor I will make at minimum $50,000 per month, which will afford me the ability to have a great impact in the earth with my philanthropic efforts and have a comfortable lifestyle, where I can spend quality time with my family at my leisure.*

IMPLEMENTATION INTENTION

Unfortunately, whenever a goal is set, there will be inevitable obstacles to overcome. When the proverbial hurdle gets in your way, what contingencies do you have in place for either prevention or correction from stumbling and falling? Put differently, how are you going to do what you say you are going to do? One successful model to follow is called "Implementation Intention."

The setting of a goal is called "goal intention," but the effective initiation of actions to carry out a goal is called "implementation intention." Remember earlier when I said that "good intentions are outweighed by poor actions"? Well here is where it applies. The things you desire, the things you want to do, the goals you set are really nothing more than well-meaning intentions. Without a strategy for execution, this is really nothing more than a wish, and you know how I feel about wishing.

Here is an excerpt from a blog post by Marelisa Fabrega, The Key to Goal Success: Setting Implementation Intentions:[30]

> *A goal is a desired outcome. When you set a goal, you're giving yourself instructions to perform certain behaviors in order to achieve your desired outcome. Unfortunately, most people fail to follow the instructions that they give themselves.*
>
> *While goals specify what you intend to achieve, implementation intentions specify the behavior you intend to take and the situational context in which you intend to take said behavior.*

There are two different aspects you need to consider when setting implementation intentions:

---

[30] Fabrega, Marelisa. The Key To Goal Success: Setting Implementation Intentions, 2013.
https://daringtolivefully.com/implementation-intentions

1. Identify the action that you're going to take to achieve your goal, and how you'll know when to take it.

2. Identify possible obstacles to goal-achievement, and how you'll deal with them.

Implementation intentions specify the what, when, and where. They are written in an "if-then" format. With implementation intentions, you're planning ahead of time the specific action that you're going to take in order to achieve your goals, as well as, when and where you're going to carry out said action. You're also creating a plan on how to continue moving forward, even when an obstacle presents itself.

FIVE STEPS TO MEET YOUR G.O.A.L.S.

(assuming the SMART Goals are already written)

❖ **G**et going

(Only action leads to accomplishment)

❖ **O**vercome obstacles

(Via organization of objectives)

❖ **A**djust your actions

(Along the way accordingly)

❖ **L**earn and leverage

(Meaning put your new knowledge to use)

❖ **S**ee Success

(F.O.C.U.S. - Follow One Course Until Successful)

SERVE YOUR WAY TO SUCCESS

"The services we provide are all things that people need, regardless of what's happening in the economy, which is what has made us resilient over time. We want to drive growth by providing a superior service in a high-quality way that's easily accessible. I'm excited about our future. Call it the road to success."
— Robert Gillette
(CEO of ServiceMaster)

This quote came from an article in *Fortune* magazine (circa March 2016 edition) and it is the perfect summation of the attitude and philosophy one must possess if they are to be successful in business as well as leadership. Not enough can be said about the importance of service as it relates to success, especially from a Biblical perspective.

"Put yourself aside, and help others get ahead. Don't be obsessed with getting your own advantage. Forget yourselves long enough to lend a helping hand."
— Philippians 2:4 (MSG)

A focus on serving means the one part of the business that you make personal. Don't just see prospects, see people and how the service you provide, or offer, can have a positive impact on their lives. Be relational, not transactional.

Relational (how you can serve them) versus Transactional (how you can charge them).

Create a win/win. Be a Blessing to others while getting paid in the process. When you focus on the things of God, then God focuses on the things of you. Zig Ziglar once said, "The best way to get what you want is to help enough other people get what they want."

The best business is not profitable because of what it sells to people, the best business is profitable because of how it serves people.

IF YOU REALLY WANT TO SUCCEED

THEN
SERVE YOUR WAY TO SUCCESS

MPOWER ME

CHAPTER 9

Get On "A" Ship

"There once was this man drowning in the middle of the sea. He prayed and said, 'God please save me.' He swam as much as he could and got tired after a little while. That's when a rowboat came by and said, 'Sir, do you need any help?' he said, 'No, God will save me.' He swam as much as he could and got tired after a little while. That's when a speedboat came by and said, 'Sir, do you need any help?' He said, 'No, God will save me.' He swam as much as he could and got tired after a little while. That's when a yacht came by and said, 'Sir, do you need any help?' He said, 'No, God will save me.' He swam as much as he could and got tired after a little while he sank, drowned and died. Once he got to heaven he said, 'God why didn't you save me?' The Lord said, 'I tried three times.'"

HOW WILL YOU GET THERE?

I tell this story because it is a wonderful example of how unrealistic our expectations of God are and how realistic God's expectations of us are.

Let me explain: this man found himself drowning, and he had an unrealistic expectation that God was going to reach His Holy Hand down from Heaven, take him out of the wate,r and place him on dry land. All the while, to his own detriment, he missed the obvious reality that was right in front of his face. Three different boats cam,e but he failed to take advantage of every opportunity presented to him.

Could it be that we have an unrealistic expectation of how we are going to get out of a situation, and we fail to notice what is right in front of us?

For instance, we are drowning in debt, and we pray God gives us money.

God sends ideas, creative solutions, and full-blown business opportunities. We say "no," and scoff at all of this. Then we say, "God, why have you not answered my prayer yet?" Then God says, *"I tried."*

What do you think Deuteronomy 8:18 means *"...He giveth thee the power to get Wealth"?*

God can do anything. But he has orchestrated it so that if He is going to move in our life, He will do so in the natural realm from His spiritual vantage point. We sometimes believe that by dreaming, hoping, and even wishing, God will do something powerful to save us from our situation. Yet we fail to notice the opportunities that are presented to us, because we don't see God doing it "that way" in our lives. We want God to move, but we have a preconceived, specific way of how He should go about it.

> *"And straightway Jesus constrained his disciples to 'get into a ship,'*
> *and to go before Him unto the other side."*
> **— Matthew 14:22**

When we look at the scripture above, the one thing it lacks is specificity.

Jesus was very general in His instructions. He told His disciples to go to "the other side" and pick any boat to get there.

Remember in Chapter 7, I said, "The how is up to you." I reinforced that notion with Psalms 1:3 by pointing out *"whatsoever you do will prosper."* I bring that up because it certainly applies here. God is not as concerned with your means or methods (as long as it is not unethical), as much as He is with you making it to "the other side."

God is essentially saying, "Here is where you are, there is where I want you to be, now you pick a vehicle to get there."

What is your vehicle to get to the other side?

For the sake of conversation, let's just say "the other side" represents success.

We are so consumed with the destination that we rarely take time to look at the vehicle that will get us there. If we go back to the story of the drowning man, we see he was so concerned with the fact that God was going to save him, that he failed to look at the way God was trying to save him. In his mind, he had a specific way he thought God was going to do it or through a specific vehicle. He thought God was going to use His hand to reach down and grab him. But when God sent other vehicles, he laughed at the notion of those because they were not what he had in mind.

Here is what I believe God wants us to get from Matthew 14:22: "...*get into A ship...*" It's not about *THE* vehicle, it's about having *A* vehicle.

Too many people are waiting on *THE* ship instead of getting on *A* ship.

The ship represents an opportunity or a vehicle to get to the other side. God said that He gave you the power to get there, and He is not as concerned about the how as much as He is concerned with you making it to the "Other Side." God is not theoretical but practical. He always has a plan to provide for His purpose, or more commonly stated, "There is always provision for the vision."

CREATE CLARITY

How do you go from an image in your mind to it becoming a reality manifested?

Make it so crystal clear that it compels you to action.

Clarity is critical for success in any endeavor as it dictates your ability to arrive at your destination. Lack of clarity is the equivalent of trying to drive across the country with the windshield covered. It is not hard to see that you will run into many problems (pun intended). Creating clarity allows you to not only know where you are going but to also see where you are going and adjust accordingly. Creating clarity is another way of saying - be clear about your vision.

> *"Where there is no vision, the people perish."*
> **— Proverbs 29:18**

A real vision mandates a roadmap. We get that in Habakkuk 2:2:

- ❖ "Write the vision." (Imagination, Innovation, Ideas, Ingenuity)

- ❖ Make it "plain." (Information; convert it to Instructions)

- ❖ "Run" that readeth it. (Implementation)

I once heard someone say, "It is not a vision until it is written. If it is not written, then it is just a wish." A vision that is written down decides upon a destination and gives direction on how you will get there.

Please do not confuse the word "how" with "whole." Often, we get stuck on how things are going to happen because we don't see or understand the whole plan or way it will get done. Do not trouble yourself with that. When I say "…gives directions on how you will get there…," I mean God will always show you the first steps. Therefore, go as far as you can see; and when you get there, you will see how to go further.

Imagine you are in New York and you want to drive to California. While in New York, you cannot see California, but you punch it into the GPS as you decide upon it as your destination, and the GPS will give you directions on how to get there. While you are driving, more directions get revealed, as you go towards it, more roads appear.

There are three Types of Vision:

1. Hindsight through Reflection
2. Insight through Introspection
3. Foresight through Projection

There is a fourth type of vision, which is oversight through subjection. Subject yourself to the counsel of a Mentor or Coach to help uncover blind spots that will further advance you in your journey quickly. I cannot stress enough how important it is to have a mentor or a coach. There is an old proverb that says, "Treat a person as they are, and they will remain as they are, but treat a person as they could or should be, and they will become who they could or should be." This is what mentoring and coaching do for you—they help you become who you could or should be. That is the power of vision in creating clarity.

The four Objectives of Clarity:

1. Clarity creates Conviction – An undying belief that you will succeed.

2. Clarity creates Confidence – "Risks come from not knowing what you are doing," (Raymond Reddington from the NBC Series, *Blacklist*). Confidence comes from competence. When you know that you know what you are doing, your confidence is at its highest.

3. Clarity creates Certainty – Become clear about your objectives. Describe what they look like. Define what it means to you. See yourself living it. Feel yourself being it. Get certain about whether you have achieved it or not. Come up with a compelling "why." The more often and the more effectively you are about being clear on what you want, the more certain it is that you will have it.

4. Clarity creates Commitment – See it so you can make it, then make it how you see it.

GET INTO "A" SHIP

When it comes to getting on a ship, you must connect your purpose with something practical. Give your versatility a vehicle. You must be open-minded about how you can get to the other side.

Some of the top businesses to become financially wealthy, (in no particular order):

1. Real Estate
2. Sales
3. Investments (such as Stocks and Trading)
4. Financial Services
5. Network Marketing
6. Affiliate Marketing
7. Online Business (creating Digital Products)
8. E-Commerce
9. Consultancy (and Coaching)
10. Traditional Business

Certainly, this is not an exhaustive list. Many opportunities exist, hence the reason for creative thought as to how you can take advantage.

John O. Jones (my mentor) told me there are five things you want in a successful business opportunity (he was referring to an MLM Company, but it could apply to any business).

1. Is it in a Growing Industry?
2. Is it a Reputable Company?
3. Do they have an Excellent Compensation Plan?
4. Do they offer Competitive Services?
5. Can they put quality people around you?

Again, he was telling me this regarding Multi-Level-Marketing, but truthfully these are all qualifying questions you should ask whether you are getting into an existing business or starting your own.

CREATE YOUR OWN ECONOMY

"Hands that don't want to work make you poor.
But hands that work hard bring wealth to you."
— **Proverbs 10:4 (NIRV)**

Work is the sacrifice for success.

It is a prerequisite for wealth—you don't get wealth without work. There is no magic pill to take, then you make a wish and become wealthy. No matter your enterprise, whatever the endeavor, to be an entrepreneur takes effort, and a lot of it.

What must be considered is what you will work on.

There are three things you want to take into consideration when you are trying to decide what to do for work. Everyone must work because "if you don't work you don't eat." (2 Thes. 3:10)

When it comes to Entrepreneurship, ask yourself, "To Be or Not to Be, that is the question."? The answer to these three things will decide if you become an entrepreneur or not:

1. Do you want to control your time by being an entrepreneur or have your time controlled by an entrepreneur?

2. Do you want to make a lot of money working as an entrepreneur or make a little money working for an entrepreneur? (i.e., profits vs. wages)

3. Do you want to work for yourself as an entrepreneur or work for someone else who is an entrepreneur?

No matter the best job you can think of working for the best company with the best benefits, if you go to the top of that food chain past the CEO, there will be an entrepreneur who is working for himself, who makes a lot of money, and who controls his time. You decide what to do with your three most precious commodities: Time, Energy (via Work), and Money, you can Invest, Spend, or Waste them.

I decided to invest mine by being an entrepreneur. You can spend yours working at a good job if you so choose and continue to waste your potential, but hey, the choice is yours.

Once you make the right decision, let's figure out what type of entrepreneur you want to be. Do you want to be the entrepreneur who is always working (even though you work for yourself), making no or too little money (even though you could be making a lot), or with no time (even though you control it)?

As you can see, even if you make the right decision (to be an entrepreneur), you can still go in the wrong direction (meaning go about it the wrong way) if you are not careful. That is why the MPOWER philosophy is so important to utilize. When you begin to put all this together, Elevating your Mind, Educating yourself on Methods, and Evaluating your Model— you ask the right questions, to get the right answers, and commit yourself to the right opportunity, so that you get the right success (i.e., Good Success)

Here is something to think about: most of Jesus' disciples were entrepreneurs.

Ultimately, what I wanted to communicate with this chapter is when Jesus told his disciples to "get into a ship," His point was for them to get to "the other side."

What is "the other side"?

That is a question you must answer for yourself, but let me impress this upon you: the other side represents your best life. Anything else is less life.

Do something that creates value, and income will follow. The more value you create, the more income you will make. After you get to the other side then you can pursue other passions and interests.

MPOWER ME

CHAPTER 10

Launch Out Into The Deep

"They that go down to the sea in ships, that do business in great waters.
These see the works of the Lord, and his wonders in the deep."
— Psalm 107:23-24

I am sure you may already know that "launch out in the deep" is a biblical reference from Luke 5:1-11, which we will go into greater detail later in this chapter. Before we go there, let's just look at the statement at face value alone.

If I come to you and say, "Launch out into the deep," this could have several different implications. I believe the first implication is very simply this: "launch out into the deep" is another way of asking the question, "What is your commitment level?"

That is essentially what Jesus was asking Peter when he told him to launch out into the deep.

How do I know Jesus questioned his commitment to success? Because to say "launch out into the deep" also implies, "You didn't go far enough."

Jesus followed up the command with, *"Let down your nets for a draught."* (Luke 5:4) The main implication here is, "Are you willing to sacrifice everything you've got; are you willing to give it all in order to succeed?"

So, let's put that all together: *launch out into the deep* and *let down your nets for a draught,* means, "Are you totally committed to go as far as necessary and give it everything you've got in order to turn your situation around"?

The resounding answer should be, YES!

> *"When you want to succeed as bad as you want to breathe, then you'll be successful."*
> — **Eric Thomas**
> *("The HipHop Preacher")*

Here is the truth of the matter, *"Toiling all night long and catching nothing,"* comes from doing small things in a shallow place, only by launching out into the deep will you see God move.

THE DETRIMENT OF DECISIONS

The power of decision is most important to comprehend, because in the moment of decision, things can change for better or worse. The decisions you make (or don't make) can literally determine or destroy your destiny. Never have such a blind ambition to get to where you're going that you lose sight of where you are.

Are you guilty of knowing what moves to make, but not fully understanding all the ramifications of that move?

This is what I mean when I say, "Daily Decisions Dictate Destiny." What you do daily will determine your destination. Any step you take at any given moment can make or break your life. Time will prove it to be a benefit or a burden. Daily decisions can be seemingly insignificant, or they could be detrimental. This should give cause for pause. This is why the Bible states, *"Count the costs." (Luke 14:28).* More importantly, when it comes to the small decisions we must make, maybe a better scripture is, *"The little foxes destroy the vine." (Song of Solomon 2:15).*

Therefore, you need to know the difference between strategic faith versus stupid faith.

❖ Strategic Faith says, "Move when God says move and step on something." Think about when Peter was walking on the water at the word of Jesus (Matthew 14:28-29).

❖ Stupid Faith is best described when the devil was tempting Jesus to step off the cliff onto nothing (Matthew 4:6). The devil even twisted scripture to get Jesus to make a false faith move.

Maybe you can relate?

Do not psych yourself out on pseudo faith that causes you to put hope in something that cannot save you once you step out there. Falsely thinking you are confident that something will work when in fact it is your own ego and arrogance.

Bishop TD Jakes once said, "There is a fine line between arrogance and confidence."

"For I bear them record that they have a zeal of God, but not according to knowledge. For they being ignorant of God's righteousness, and going about to establish their own righteousness, have not submitted themselves unto the righteousness of God."
— Romans 10:2-3

"Enthusiasm without knowledge is no good; haste makes mistakes."
— Proverbs 19:2 (NLT)

WHAT IS GOD'S WILL?

Have you ever prayed to know what God's will is for a situation? You have an important decision that you need to make, and you are praying fervently for God to speak to you? Ever been there? You hear nothing, and after all that prayer and maybe even some fasting, you still feel like it is a 50/50 shot in the dark that you hope works out? Sound familiar? I know the feeling all too well!

Then one day it hit me: most of the time when we are praying for God's will, we fail to see how God moves. Think about how He has orchestrated things in your life. Think about the way He has made for you, the doors He opened and even the doors He closed. These are all indicators of what His will is. God's will is never disconnected from God's ways.

Look at this scripture:

"Trust in the Lord with all thine heart; and lean not unto thine own understanding. In all thy ways acknowledge Him, and He shall direct thy paths."
— Proverbs 3:5-6 (Emphasis added)

Notice it says, "… He shall DIRECT thy paths." This literally means He (God) will make a path for you. That is where the old church saying comes from, "He will make a way out of no way." This action is spelled out in *Isaiah 45:2: "I will go before you and make the rough places smooth." (NASB)*

This is why we must trust God, because:

*"The steps of a good man are **ordered by the Lord:** and He delighteth in his way."*
— Psalm 37:23

Again, look at His action: "ordered by the Lord…"

When I was praying, Lord, what is your will? I was expecting Him to say *His will*, when what He did was *show me His way*. This simply meant that I had to be sensitive to the Spirit and watch God move. Then I would know what His will was.

When God put it all together for me, He summed it up like this:

"Where the Hand of God is shown, the Will of God is known."

God shows His hand in many ways, and we should obey Him when He gives us clear instructions. However, I want to point out three ways that He communicates *that are not as easily recognized* as God.

1. **Ideas** – Something you think of that seems like the leading of the Lord. Now, not every idea is a good idea and certainly not every idea is a God idea. So, what is the difference between a bad idea and a good idea? A bad idea will be a burden, whereas a good idea will be a blessing. Further still, what is the difference between a good idea and a God idea? A good idea will always bless you, whereas a God idea will always bless others.

2. **Intuition** – Something you know you should do. Typically, intuition is mixed with ingenuity. So not only is it something that you know you should do, but when it is from God then you will also know how to get it done.

3. **Instances** – Something happens that you know is a God-move. Some sort of incident occurs that is obviously God getting your attention. Now, the way He goes about doing that may not always feel good, but it will end up being for your good. Look at Romans 8:28, which is explained by 1 Peter 5:6-11.

What is God's will? That is a great question. We know He does not always express it in words. Therefore, it is important that you stay in tune with the *Ideas, Intuition,* and *Instances* in your life that speak to a larger purpose, because these are ways that God will tell you His will.

Life is a series of seasons, stages, and situations. Your response in those times of trials, tribulations, and temptations will dictate how long each of them will last. It is critical that you learn how to handle those changes, cycles, and circumstances, to use them to your advantage.

LAUNCH OUT INTO THE DEEP

"And it came to pass, that, as the people pressed upon him to hear the word of God, he stood by the lake of Gennesaret. And saw two ships standing by the lake: but the fishermen were gone out of them and were washing their nets. And he entered into one of the ships, which was Simon's, and prayed him that he would thrust out a little from the land. And he sat down and taught the people out of the ship. Now when he had left speaking, he said unto Simon, Launch out into the deep, and let down your nets for a draught."

— Luke 5:1-4

The scripture referenced here shows Jesus walking onto a scene where some discouraged fishermen were *"washing their nets."* This statement is the scriptural equivalent of *"quitting."* There is no worse situation than trying to motivate someone who has essentially given up. Typically, whatever positivity you try to interject, they will respond with a negative excuse as to why it won't work. So, how did Jesus get them to go back out? He changed their *Hope*, their *How* and their *Hunger*.

❖ He gave them a new "Hope" — *And He sat down and **taught** the people out of the ship.*

His method for change began with His message. It was in this message that I believe He gave them new hope not to quit. Consequently, they were willing to follow Jesus' instructions. Whatever He said in this powerful message compelled them to obey what He told them, even if they thought it was against their better judgment. Ultimately, if you want to see your situation shift, either change your expectations or your environment. Jesus changed their Expectations first. I believe Jesus exposed them to new possibilities in the message He taught.

Exposure creates Expectation. You cannot want a thing until you first know that it exists.

We already established in Chapter 4 that Awareness is the first step toward achievement. Whatever Jesus taught the disciples made them aware that more was available to them. If that is true for them, then it is true for you also. It is critical that you realize that there is more in store for you. Abandon all notions of quitting and giving up. Throwing in the proverbial towel is not an option. *Frustration is a call to action.* Either change your Perspective (the way you look at it) or your Procedure (what you are doing that's not working). Jesus changed both by also changing their Environment.

❖ He gave them a new "How" — *Launch out into the deep.*

Too many times, we are victims of circumstances, all predicated upon the environment in which we find ourselves. The changing of one's environment means the possibility of going beyond the limitations. Never make decisions based solely on circumstances. Decisions should be made despite and not influenced by circumstances because decisions made despite circumstances are a choice based on convictions. Decisions influenced by circumstances are a choice based on conditions. You can always change your conditions, if you just get creative – *Launch Out into the Deep.*

❖ He gave them a new "Hunger" — *Let down your nets for a draught.*

"You Gotta Be Hungry."
— Les Brown

Hunger is your drive to thrive! Peter was hungry again (because of the message he heard) but he was uneasy (some may even say unwilling) to do what was necessary to fulfill his hunger. The reason why is because he remembered what happened the last time he threw his nets and he should have caught something yet didn't.

The problem is he wanted to do it, but he also did not want to do it simultaneously. Peter's response is very telling of his mindset at the time.

"And Simon answering said unto him, Master, we have toiled all the night, and have taken nothing: nevertheless, at thy word I will let down the net."
— Luke 5:5

This was Peter's issue. He was washing his nets and ready to quit, then heard a powerful message that inspired him to act. In other words, he was hungrier now than before.

"Launch out into the deep and let down your nets for a draught (a catch)."

Have you ever wanted to do something, yet you didn't do it and don't know why you didn't do it? Have you ever felt like something would work and would not work at the same time? This state of flux where we "do and don't" at the same time puts us in a quandary because our minds have a difficult time working out this dilemma.

Our minds serve two primary functions, which are to: protect us and provide for us; keep us happy while keeping us away from what will hurt us (albeit physical or otherwise); fulfill our desire for more pleasure and less pain, with little disappointment and a lot of delight. When the mind finds itself in a situation where the outcome can be both at the same time, it presents a complex dichotomy for the mind. Where if you do this thing, it could make you happy, but if it does not work, it could also cause you more hurt.

In the field of psychology, cognitive dissonance *is the mental discomfort (psychological stress) experienced by a person who simultaneously holds two or more contradictory and inconsistent beliefs, ideas, or thoughts in their mind, especially as relating to behavioral decisions and attitude change.*[31] I believe it is very important for you to know this because I feel it affects you also.

When we hold contradicting beliefs in our minds (*I want to do it, but I don't know if I can*); when something inspires you and you want to take action, but then come up with self-sabotaging excuses as to why it won't work—this

---

[31] Cognitive Dissonance. WikiQuote. Last accessed 2018. https://en.wikiquote.org/wiki/Cognitive_dissonance

keeps you stuck where you may give some effort but not the full effort and it is causes other problems in your life.

THE NET BRAKE

"Ambition only becomes Fruition when you Learn to Listen."
— **Roger Daye**

Because of Peter's cognitive dissonance, he chose disobedience, which almost led to total disaster. Jesus gave very clear instructions to let down the *NETS* (Luke 5:4), but Peter responded with an excuse, which led to little effort. He said, "Master, we have toiled all night and have taken nothing; nevertheless, at Thy Word I will let down the *NET.*" (Luke 5:5)

"Do all things without murmurings and disputings."
— **Philippians 2:14**

Complaining is being Consistently Critical of your Current Condition while Continuously giving Power to the Problem.

When we don't do it God's way, you can expect problems. Because Peter did not follow the plan totally, he had issues that could have been avoided had he been completely obedient in the first place.

Jesus said nets (plural), Peter said net (singular). Partial obedience is full disobedience, which creates a preventable problem.

Proper planning and preparation prevent poor performance. Anytime we make excuses and are unwilling to put forth the full effort because of past hurts and/or failures we can expect to see problems that could have been prevented. Jesus wanted Peter to give it everything he had, yet Peter chose not to give it his all and his net broke.

Some of us are suffering from the detriments of our own decisions. When it comes to decisions, you have to ask not only WHAT it will cost you, but also

HOW it will cost you if you don't do it. This is called "Opportunity Cost." What are you missing out on because you did not make the decision to do something to the fullest and absolute best of your ability? One must be willing to run the risk of losing to reach the reward of gaining.

How many times in our own lives have we been given a unique opportunity, but because of excuses, we didn't put forth the full effort and give it our all, only to look back at that situation with regret, because we know we missed a chance to take our best shot? Peter was frustrated because they had fished all night long and caught nothing. Do not be defined by your conditions or circumstances, and do not allow your frustrations to lead you to a fear of failure.

F.E.A.R. is nothing more than…

- Foolishness
- Effectively
- Aborting
- Rewards

Too often we allow ourselves to make foolish excuses as to why a thing will fail, then we prove that prophecy right by giving foolish efforts which leads to that failure, effectively aborting any hope of the real reward God was trying to give us if we would have responded with faith and not foolishness. Then we wonder why we feel like a fool, because we attempt to console ourselves with, "I knew it wouldn't work anyway, but at least I tried."

There are three main frustrations that lead to failing, and all three are intensified by F.E.A.R:

1. Denials (fear of rejection)

When we experience this frustration, we have prepared ourselves for a negative response, while never seeing the potential for a positive outcome. But we must rather, only see the positive outcome (and not accept negative responses) then — we will not allow any denial to get in the way of us getting the thing we desire.

2. Distractions (fear of prioritizing)

When we experience this frustration, we give what we feel are legitimate reasons (i.e., excuses) as to why we can't get something done. When the truth is, you have not properly prioritized. Think about it like this: if you give up the thing you feel you don't have, then you will get the thing you want. If you say you don't have the time, money, or energy to get it done, that means precisely that you should *take the time, money, or energy to get it done*. You must sow where you want to go and grow. Because if you do, then you will have more time, money, or energy once the endeavor is finished and has succeeded. But it will never succeed if you keep getting distracted by some perceived lack.

3. Delays (fear of decision)

When we experience this frustration, it is because we failed to make a decision we knew we should have made, within a certain window of time. Do you think it is a coincidence that the first thing Jesus said to Peter after He finished teaching was, "Launch out into the deep?" I do not. Jesus reinforced a decision Peter knew he should have made earlier—to not give up. But, because of Denials and Distractions, Peter was delayed in getting what God had in store for him. Make a decision and live with the results. However, when you decide, do not do it half-heartedly; give it everything you've got. Commit yourself to seeing the outcome you desire - letting nothing stop you.

The "Do's and Don'ts" when it comes to God's instructions:

❖ Do it *immediately*. Incorporate it into whatever you currently have going on. The implication is that His word is always NOW unless He says otherwise.

❖ Don't *ignore* it. Increase your sensitivity to the Spirit to distinguish between God's voice and other voices (especially your own) that attempt to drown Him out.

❖ Do *innovate*. Get creative! You have what you need now to get to where you want to be later. There is always something you have at your disposal (in your current situation) that can be leveraged (Exodus 4:2).

❖ Don't *insult* God with excuses (Exodus 4:10-14). An excuse is nothing more than a well-planned lie. The biggest cause of regret and failure is excuses.

PRACTICAL PESSIMISM

Peter said, *"Master we have toiled all night long and have taken nothing."* (Luke 5:5) I do want to give Peter some credit here (because he gets picked on a lot in this story), at least this statement shows he is taking into consideration the business ramifications of what Jesus has just asked him to do (in case it fails again).

What I am getting ready to tell you now will seem as if I am contradicting myself, but I am not. Until now I have told you how fear gets in the way of us doing the thing we know we should do. While the power of positive thinking is a positive thing, it is possible to be positive to a fault. Sometimes people do not like to face facts. For that type of person, it can be difficult to see what is wrong. Why? Because they are only picturing the positive by looking through rose-colored glasses, to the detriment of neglecting the truth within the negative. Here is what is positive about the negative: it shows room for improvement. There is nothing worse than being blindsided by something for which you could have been prepared.

There is a functionality in fear, if used properly, called *practical pessimism*. Contemplate the downside, which, when put into practice, helps you create a plan to prosper by using the negative aspects of a potential outcome as motivation to avoid that very outcome. Therefore, you expect the unexpected, so you can *"innovate your way out of it,"* as Jeff Bezos (CEO of Amazon) said of potential problems and possible setbacks.

Biblically put, we are encouraged to *"Count up the Costs."* (Luke 14:28)

The consistent question we must ask ourselves is, "what can go wrong"? Not as a justification to stop but as motivation to keep going. By preparing for the worst, you achieve your best. It was Susan Jeffers who said, "Feel the fear and do it anyway." Use your fear as fuel to push past the pain of your current circumstances and create your better tomorrow today.

EVENTUALITIES PLAN

Eventualities Plan is a business term where you create a written-out strategy to be ready for identifiable issues. In other words, it means to use professional hindsight, insight, and foresight to anticipate possible or potential occurrences and have a contingency in place for each scenario so that you can lessen, minimize and contain any negative impact or damage. It is a fancy way of asking, "What is your Plan B?"

There is no accomplishment without adjustment. I would be remiss and doing you a disservice if I didn't point out, Peter came up with a "Plan B."

Peter saw that his original system (of throwing out the one net) was not working like he thought, so he had to adjust, *"and they beckoned unto their partners, that they should come and help them."* (Luke 5:7) Why is this important to point out? Well, what if it works? How will you handle it? What is your contingency for growth? Clearly, Peter had a plan for failure; that's why he only threw out the one net. But he was surprised when he succeeded, and his success almost turned into failure because he almost lost what he had just caught.

A good word to describe what I am talking about here is "expansion." This is what Jesus was talking about when He said, *"Don't put new wine into old wineskins, lest it burst"* (Luke 5:37). The old wineskin won't be able to handle the expansion of the new wine. If what you are endeavoring to do is in the will of God, then you better prepare for "expansion."

Most people plan for failure, but they don't plan for success. As you grow, your system must be able to grow, too. If your system doesn't have room for growth and expansion, then it is the wrong system. Be sure to have a system that can scale with you and simply adjust where necessary.

FROM FAILURE SEE SUCCESS

"Failures are the bricks that pave your way to success."
— Christian Mickelsen

"Failures are nothing more than the turns one must take to reach their destination, for every time I fail, I will take another turn until I arrive where I want to be."
— Anonymous

Failure, in this instance, means the disciples knew where the fish were not. Now, the key is to learn from that and try again, not live in that and give up. Too often, we face failure and see it as the end of the road. After facing adversity, you will commence *"washing your nets."*

Failure awaits those who do not apply life lessons when they are taught. The failure is there as an indicator to let you know where things went wrong and how to learn from your mistakes. This makes failure a life lesson in and of itself. It is there to teach us how not to fail next time. Success is always beyond the point of failure. You must go through failure to get to success.

EQUALITY OF EFFORT

Peter's response to Jesus' command sheds some light on the character of these fishermen. When Jesus said, *"Launch out into the deep and let down your nets for a draught,"* Peter replied, "Master, we have toiled all night long." This statement shows their resolve, to be sure. But resiliency alone will not change reality.

Perhaps you have heard the definition of insanity is: *doing the same thing over and over yet expecting a different result.* While being resilient is certainly a trait to be admired, you will need more than this to change your situation. The men had already expended a great deal of energy and effort, but effort without effectiveness only equals exhaustion.

It is critical that you understand the Law "Equality of Effort," which states that the same effort it takes to do a good thing is the same effort it takes to do a greater thing. Effort in God is measured by effectiveness (John 21:5-6). Therefore, if you are going to "toil all night," don't let it be for shallow things. Instead, "launch out into the deep" and give it all you've got. Effort is nothing if you're not effective, but make sure you are putting that effort towards something worth the sacrifice.

PREFER PARTNERSHIPS

"And he called other little ships that were with him."
— Luke 5:7

Creating connections is what will really catapult you to the next level. True success comes through collaboration not competition.

My definition of collaboration is:

"We" is always better than "Me."

When you only compete, you are working against a perceived opponent. To work against instead of working with automatically puts you in a posture of negativity, which means for you to win someone else must lose. This isolates you from greater creativity, because you become an island unto yourself. To cut yourself off such as this will eventually cause stagnation, because growth stops.

The model we see in scripture is different because it poses a question like, *Can two walk together, except they be agreed? Amos 3:3.* The answer certainly is NO. But why would this question even be important? Because God has mandated:

"Again, I say unto you, that if two of you shall agree on earth as touching anything that they shall ask, it shall be done for them of my Father which is in heaven. For where two or three are gathered together in my name, there am I in the midst of them."
— Matthew 18:19-20

Therefore, we can see when we are friends instead of foes, the power of partnership comes into play because according to this scripture; only through partnering will we see God's presence where He fulfills this promise.

"Thou wilt shew me the path of life: in thy presence is fullness of joy; at thy right hand there are pleasures for evermore."
— Psalm 16:11

This is what we want because when God shows up, He shows out and shows off on "our" behalf.

*The uniqueness of our vision when **We Accept***

*The calling of God to unify our vision when **We Connect***

*Will bring about our vision as **We Step***

Two is always better than one, because one has always been too small a number to have a real impact. One can get something started, but it will take a lot more than one to finish.

Deuteronomy 32:30 states, *"if 1 can chase a 1,000, then two can chase 10,000,"* which essentially means, when we work with others instead of seeing them as opposition, our agreement increases our achievement tenfold.

MPOWER ME

CHAPTER 11

Go To The Sea and Cast a Hook

God's expectation of you is based upon how you have been equipped.

Expectation of a person is only reasonable if they have been equipped with and know how to use the tools at their disposal to meet such an expectation.

Example:

It is unfair to expect an automobile mechanic to build a house like he is a carpenter.

He will be ill-equipped, and all the tools at his disposal are for what he knows how to do.

You have been given a gift or talent, and the solution to your struggle is through strategic stewardship of that gift or talent.

In the Kingdom of God, **the Pathway to Prosperity is through the Perfection of your Purpose.**

"Notwithstanding, lest we should offend them, go thou to the sea, and cast a hook, and take up the fish that first cometh up; and when thou hast opened his mouth, thou shalt find a piece of money: that take and give unto them for me and thee."
— Matthew 17:27

Getting on "A" ship is the equivalent of getting into an industry, but casting in a hook is the equivalent of picking a niche in that industry.

A niche is a place, job, status, or activity for which a person or thing is best fitted: the situation in which a business's products or services can succeed by being sold to a certain kind or group of people.

What is your "Hook"?

The sea represents the marketplace, and the hook represents what is unique about you that you can monetize and offer to the marketplace as something of value.

What is your specialty? What is your area of expertise?

A Better question is what is your Purpose? We are going to expound on this more in just a bit; but the question becomes, what are you good/great at?

If you don't know, then start with your area of gifting.

Too many times, people get their Purpose, their Calling, and their Gifting mixed up.

- ❖ Your *Purpose* is what you were built to do. It is the "why" you exist.

- ❖ Your *Calling* is to a certain place, people, or project, at a certain point in time. to fulfill your purpose.

- ❖ Your *Gift* is how you get your purpose and calling accomplished.

Your destiny is short for a God-designed destination.

Let's use the example of a car again. Your "purpose" is the driver of the car.

The car itself is the gift (vehicle) given to you by God, to get you to where God wants you to go.

Where you go is wherever He is calling you to (could also be stated as your destiny).

I can even throw this in for added understanding: your passion is fuel for the vehicle/gift.

DIVINE DESIGN

"I will praise thee; for I am fearfully and wonderfully made:
marvelous are thy works."
— Psalms 139:14

Do you know you have been built to be blessed, engineered to excel, and shaped for success?

You were destined by divine design to do mighty exploits. (Daniel 11:32).

"You have to be bold enough to turn your gifts into your business and be confident
enough to charge for your services. You are a business, and you were born to
succeed. Trust the process and don't just sit on the outside and look in,
Get in the game and get a piece of the pie."
— Tony Gaskins

"Make your passion your paycheck and your daydream your day job."
— Jay Shetty

The official Merriam-Webster Dictionary defines passion as *a strong feeling of enthusiasm or excitement for something or about doing something; a strong liking or desire for or devotion to some activity, object, or concept; intense emotion compelling action.*

But I like the more relevant Urban Dictionary's definition: *Passion is when you put more energy into something than is required to do it. It is more than just enthusiasm or excitement; passion is ambition that is materialized into action to put as much heart, mind, body, and soul into something as is possible.*

Typically, when people think about something they are passionate about they tend to think of hobbies like video games, doing some craft, or playing or watching a sport like golf, football, baseball, basketball, or bowling.

Those are all great things to pass the time, but that is more so for recreation.

However, passion really is more of an environment that elicits emotion.

It is when certain conditions come together that evoke a strong emotion in you to want to do something in that moment and create some change to a condition or circumstance.

When asked what you are passionate about, the truth is you want to see change for the better in some area.

But, passion and purpose are always connected therefore, *PURPOSE*, on the other hand, is defined as *the reason why something is done or used.* It is the aim or intention of something; the feeling of being determined to do or achieve something; the aim or goal of a person: what a person is trying to do, become and so on.

We talked about *Purpose* in chapters 3 and 5, now let's go deeper.

> *"(1) Blessed is the man that walketh not in the counsel of the ungodly,*
> *nor standeth in the way of sinners, nor sitteth in the seat of the scornful.*
> *(2) But his delight is in the Law of the Lord;*
> *and in His Law doth he meditate day and night.*
> *(3) And he shall be like a tree planted by the rivers of water, that bringeth*
> *forth his fruit in his season; his leaf also shall not wither; and whatsoever he*
> *doeth shall prosper."*
> **— Psalm 1:1-3**

Here is a scripture that proves the "Power of Purpose"!

When the Bible talks about being "planted" it is talking about being "planted in your purpose". Once you are "planted in your purpose" then Prosperity comes; no matter what you do in the area of your purpose.

So you have to be anchored, rooted, and grounded in who you were created to be (via the roadmap in verses 1 and 2 [above]); in order to see true fulfillment in life.

Typically, when asked what their purpose is, people respond with, "I don't know *how to find my purpose."*

The word "find" puts the mind in a state as though your purpose is lost when nothing could be further from the truth.

Let me use this as an example to try to explain my point here:

Have you ever reached into an old jacket or an old purse and pulled money out of the pocket that you put there some time ago? Then you say to yourself, "Wow, look at what I just *found."*

But, the truth of the matter is you didn't really find it; it was there all along, you simply forgot you put it there.

That is how purpose works, you know what it is—you just forgot it.

Your purpose is not some arbitrary thing God is trying to hide from you and forcing you to look for it; your purpose simply needs to be revealed, and that happens via life's experiences.

When you review your entire life history, note what has been congruent.

When you take the time to remember the course of your life; look at the high and low times, the good and the bad times, those things that brought you pain and those things that brought you joy and peace, the negatives, the positives, the problems and the pleasures, I guarantee you will find a common denominator.

There was something that you were doing that was putting a smile on your face and when you were not doing it, you were not as happy.

What is that common recurring theme?

Answer that, and you will be on the path to revealing/remembering your purpose.

Most of the time, deep down, we already know what our purpose is or what we should be doing, but we don't see it as anything of value, so we dismiss it, and say it has to be something bigger than that. But that is the wrong way to look at it.

Purpose is a verb, not a noun. Therefore, you find your purpose by doing different things, and an indicator (of the different things you should be doing) is your gifting.

God gave you a gift to solve a problem. So don't pick a purpose, pick a problem.

You are a solution to a problem (no matter how big or small, in your eyes). Remember the Parable of the Talents; it is not about quantity, but quality.

Don't minimize the magnitude of what God has created you to do, by treating it as though it is minuscule.

Stop trying to avoid it and embrace it.

PAID FOR PURPOSE

You can be paid for your passion and purpose.

Think about that for a moment.

Most people believe it is too good to be true, but you see it all the time.

Think about movie stars, comedians, entertainers, professional athletes, and successful entrepreneurs who are all paid for their passion and purpose. For those people who do believe it, they believe it is only true for others, but not for themselves. But the truth of the matter is, you can be paid to do what you love.

Remember when I said: *"I want to Prove People can Prosper through Perfection of Purpose."*

This is what I meant.

R.E.A.L. BUSINESS vs. "REAL" JOB

Have you ever heard the term "go get a 'real' job"? Most of the time, when this is said, it is meant as an indictment on whatever you were trying to do (that they felt) was not working. Most of the time, it is said by haters, but sometimes it is said by well-meaning loved ones who are concerned that you are chasing some pipedream (to have a business of your own) will result in you being broke and homeless. So, after some time of seeing you struggle to get your business off the ground, they finally say, "You should go get a 'real' job."

Why do people forego starting their own businesses versus getting a "real job" anyway?

Most say entrepreneurship is too risky, and getting a traditional job provides stability. I disagree.

I think the threat of being fired via enforcement (if a policy is violated) is why people choose employment over entrepreneurship.

Put differently, people do not go to their job because of stability; they go because of the structure it provides.

Because you run the risk of being fired for non-productivity is why you do what you are supposed to do at your "real job." Stability should not mean someone else forcing you to take responsibility, if you are unproductive or break the company rules.

It is not that you work at a "real job," as much as it is that you work for a R.E.A.L Business:

- ❖ Relevance via Results
- ❖ Effective, Efficient, and Excellent
- ❖ Accountability for activity
- ❖ Leadership and Logistics

Most do not succeed in their entrepreneurial endeavors because they lack the "strength of structure." This means they do not treat their business like a "real job." The main difference for a lot of people who go into business for themselves and a "real job" is— their approach.

The only actual appeal of a "real job" comes from the stability that has been created via a real structure. There are consequences for actions (or the lack thereof). As a matter of fact, it is these "consequences" that make most people want to go into business for themselves anyway.

Go figure…

Most people want to be their own boss, but what type of boss would you be? If you would not be the type of boss who would fire yourself if you do not produce, then you are not cut out to be a real entrepreneur. You should just keep your "real job."

SERVICE THROUGH SALES

Remember when I said the 3rd point of MPOWER was to Evaluate Your Model, "Serve your way to Success." Well here is one way to do that. If you are going to succeed in business, you will have to get over your apprehensions about selling.

Selling is a way to facilitate an automated exchange of purpose. It is the expression of your purpose for a profit. Unfortunately, most people do not see selling as a service; they see it as some slimy, greasy tactic or, at best, a necessary evil. This is not true. We need to look at selling as a successive conversation to serve your client or customer and help them achieve a desire they do not yet know they have. For example, think of the Apple iPad. Before it came out, did you think you needed it? For most, the answer is no. You didn't realize how much you needed it until it was in your life. Now, it's something you can't imagine living without. This is sales.

The Bible tells us, *Ye have not, because ye ask not.* (James 4:2). And in order to succeed in sales, you have to know "The Art of *A.S.K.*ing."

- ❖ <u>A</u>sk. It takes a certain attitude. Most people do not like the rejection, but don't look at it like that. See it as every "no" gets you closer to a "yes." In Jack Canfield's book, *The Success Principles*, he said to use the "SW" principle: Some Will, Some Won't, So What, Someone's Waiting.[32]

- ❖ <u>S</u>eek. Another place for your aptitude. This is where your gifting applies. Seek those with whom you can connect. This is necessary for what is called *"rapport."* If you do not use your gift you will be inauthentic. It is critical that you be yourself; do not sound "salesy" just have a conversation.

- ❖ <u>K</u>nock. This is the application of action. You don't sell 100% of the product(s) (be it tangible or intangible), that you don't show or share

---

[32] Canfield, Jack. The Success Principles: How to get from Where You Are to Where You Want to Be (New York City: HarperCollins Publishers; 2015); page 147

with a customer/client.[33] At least showing or sharing your product(s) means you have a shot at getting the sale or closing the deal. Your efforts will pay off if you do not quit. You must be committed to the sales process.

Jack Canfield and Mark Victor Hansen wrote a great book, *The Aladdin Factor: How to Ask for and Get What You Want in Every Area of Your Life,*[34] which I recommend you read regarding this subject.

When it comes to sales, it is critical that you build rapport as quickly as possible. A "prospect" is a prospective buyer or potential customer/client. You must overcome three hurdles before your prospect will make a purchase decision.

1. Know
2. Like
3. Trust

If they do not know you, like you, or trust you, then there will be no sale. You must get past these obstacles before they will buy. Typically, the questions they ask will be an indicator of how well you covered these areas. There is a natural progression here, and do not try to go out of order, or else you will be out of (an) order.

You may be familiar with a sales concept called the "Law of Averages," which is most commonly referred to as a "Numbers Game."

The theory is – if you talk to enough people you are bound to get a sale at some point. There definitely is some truth to that.

---

[33] Hults, Donald. Unseen Untold is Unsold: Salesmanship & Common Sense. (Indiana: Trafford Publishing; 2009); page 44

[34] Canfield, Jack and Hansen, Mark Victor. The Aladdin Factor: (New York City: Berkeley Books Publishers; 1995)

But I want to introduce the "Law of the Advantage," which takes into consideration the MPOWER philosophy and the Combination to Success.

"The yoke shall be destroyed because of the anointing."
— Isaiah 10:27

The word "yoke" in the scripture here means burden. In the Law of Averages, you must deal with the burden of going through a sometimes-arduous process before you see some success. The word anointing in the scripture means to be set apart for special use. Therefore, the burden is destroyed when you are set apart for special use.

That is your advantage over the average: "Mastery" sets you apart. Your uniqueness by way of utilizing this philosophy (i.e., MPOWER) "Mastery: People Overcome with Education & Resources" empowers you to not be average. Because you have the advantage— God has declared, **WHATSOEVER** *You do shall prosper* (Psalms 1:3).

CHILDREN, HAVE YE ANY MEAT?

*"Then Jesus saith unto them, **Children, have ye any meat?***
They answered him, No. And He said unto them,
Cast the net on the right side of the ship, and ye shall find.
They cast therefore, and now they were not able to draw it
for the multitude of fishes."
— John 21:5-6 (emphasis added)

Jesus asked His disciples a critical question, which gives us insight as to God's explicit expectation for our lives.

The first commandment after creation was to be fruitful and multiply (Genesis 1:28). Jesus cursed the fig tree because it looked fruitful but in reality, it was not (Matthew 21:19). I once heard it put this way by a friend of mine,

Carmen Stephens: *"The tree had the leaves of profession but lacked the fruit of progression."*

In other words, it was trying to fake it, but did not make it because it got cursed.

Well, there goes the "fake it, till you make it" theory. In God's sight, faking means fruitless. How about we "Faith it, till we make it" instead, which is exactly what Jesus admonished us to do.

> *"Jesus answered and said unto them, Verily I say unto you, if ye have faith, and doubt not, ye shall not only do this which is done to the fig tree, but also if ye shall say unto this mountain, be thou removed, and be thou cast into the sea; it shall be done."*
> **— Matthew 21:21**

Effort is evident because when you put forth your best effort, you produce.

Don't just try—DO!

If you give real effort, there will be real evidence.

When Jesus asked the disciples, "Have ye any meat?" He was really asking, "Are you being effective at what you are doing?"

CAST YOUR NETS ON THE RIGHT SIDE OF THE SHIP

When you hear, *"Cast your nets on the right side of the ship,"* what immediately comes to mind? The obvious answer is; I must have my nets on the wrong side of the ship, that's why whatever you are trying to do is not working.

But let's go deeper. Remember in Chapter 2 when I told you *the wealth of the wicked is laid up for the just?* This is another example of what I meant.

Let's say you picked a boat (i.e., started/gotten into a business) and it is still not working. Then cast your nets on the right side of the ship. Put differently—do something that works!

Productivity is what God wants—from the question, "children, have ye any meat?" to the parable of the talents where the wicked servant was cursed (because he didn't generate an increase). God only cares about what you are doing, to the point of finding out what the results are from what you are doing? Once He finds out these results, His admonishment is: if what you are doing is not working, then try something different. Why? As long as you are in the right place, the reward is prosperity, but if you are in the wrong place, then wealth procrastinates.

I said it before, and I will say it again: "God gave you the Power to get Wealth; if you don't have it, it is your fault."

I know it didn't feel good to hear the first time I said it, and I'm sure this feels no better, but I care too much to lie to you. In Chapter 10, I said, "effort without effectiveness equals exhaustion." (Luke 5:5). This is the equivalent of multiplying by zero; no matter how big the first number is, once it is multiplied by zero, it will equal zero still.

1000% of effort multiplied by 0% of effectiveness = "toiling all night and catching nothing."

Abandon all things that will not lead you to acquisition. Frustration is the difference between where you are and where you want to be. If you are not getting the results you desire, then change either the way you are doing it or change what you are doing entirely. Either way, your mandate from God is to "Get it Done!" Don't just be busy; switch to something that works. God cares about productivity. You will know you are being productive when you see results via prosperity.

Success is getting what you are going after. If what you are doing will not get you there, then do something else that will.

When the Bible says in Psalms 1:3, *"whatsoever you do shall prosper,"* it is with the caveat that you were planted.

Please plant this in the very essence of your being—use the "Combination to Success"—your Attitude, Aptitude, and Actions through MPOWER (i.e., Mastery of your Mentality, Methodology, and Modality) by Elevating your Mind, Educating yourself on Methods, and Evaluating your Model in order to see success happen in your life, leadership, and legacy.

Periodically, you should take inventory and ask yourself the question, "Have you any meat?" as an indicator to conduct an examination of your effectiveness. (2 Cor 13:5)

In regard to this matter, remember this…

THE MEASURING STICK FOR PRODUCTIVITY IS PROSPERITY!

MPOWER ME

CHAPTER 12

The Conclusion of The Matter

What do you believe about people?

> *"And God saw everything that He had made,*
> *and, behold, it was very good."*
> **— Genesis 1:31**

I believe that people are inherently good, but I'm not naive to the fact that people (sometimes or often, depending on who they are) do things that are bad or downright evil (depending on the severity of the act).

Still, I truly do believe for the most part people generally want to do what is right, but because they do not always know "how" they sometimes succumb to the lesser of themselves.

I believe God gives us all the opportunity to become our highest and best selves. For this reason, He dealt to every man a measure of faith (Romans 12:3).

This forms the basis for my belief that all people are inherently good, because we are made in God's image and in God's likeness (Genesis 1:26). When God blew into man's nostrils and gave us the breath of life (Genesis 2:7), He also gave us all faith. Because without faith it is impossible to please Him (Hebrews 11:6), and God has never set us up for failure. We are equally equipped to be good, which means our best selves living to our fullest potential.

Some may say, *"yet, we are bad because we were born in sin and shapen in iniquity,"* (Psalms 51:5) to which I respond, the pain in which you were born does not override the purpose for which you were created.

Have a practical perspective on your possibilities. Yes, the sky's the limit, but the Stairway to Heaven requires taking some very serious steps. The key is to learn to take the steps to climb higher while still keeping your feet firmly planted to the ground.

BE BETTER
(My Story of Emotional Implantation)

I have had a few life-altering experiences that shifted my paradigm through emotional implantation. The most notable of these experiences was the tragic death of my sister, "Danielle." Her death rocked my family to our core because it was so horrific and uncalled for. My sister was murdered by an ex-boyfriend who shot her in the head at point-blank range while she was sleeping, for absolutely no justifiable reason. This caught us all off guard, a truly horrible and traumatic experience. Danielle was not only a daughter and our sister, but she was also a mother of four; (my niece and three nephews). This only further intensified the entire situation because not only did my family and I have to deal with such a heinous act, but we also had to figure out a way to comfort and create a new normal for these children.

To make a long story short (because I could write an entire book on this ordeal), this was a major emotional implantation that really changed the trajectory of my life. She was twenty-seven years old and so very beautiful both inside and out. I had to do my sister's eulogy, and when I tried to think of the best way to honor Danielle's memory, God spoke these words to me: *"Be what she thought you were."*

My sister really looked up to me, and God essentially told me that day, *"Live up to what she looked up to."* Therefore, the message I preached was "Be Better." You may not be able to be perfect, but you can BE **BETTER**! (Isaiah 6:1-8)

This experience shifted my paradigm to truly understand purpose, and how quickly things can change. We do not have time to waste. Life is so very precious, and yet so fleeting.

> *"Whereas ye know not what shall be on the morrow. For what is your life?*
> *It is even a vapour that appears for a little time and then vanishes away."*
> **— James 4:14**

We were all born with a purpose (Jeremiah 1:5), and this needs to be the focus of our lives. To strive to be better in every relationship, in every interaction, in every endeavor, in every shape, form, and fashion. You can be better. In the famous words of French psychologist Émile Coué, tell yourself, "Day by day, in every way, I'm getting better and better." The time to be your best self is now.

Better your best. Develop a determination to go deeper, by deciding to remove distractions, through dedicating yourself to pursue destiny.

Move past money to what really matters, which is "Meaning."

Is the work that you are engaging in meaningful?

The thing which you give yourself to, the thing into which you put blood, sweat, tears, and years, is it worth it?

> *"Is there not a cause?"*
> **— 1 Samuel 17:29**

This was David's response to dealing with Goliath. There is a Goliath that God has called you to slay, and the success that comes from such a sacrifice should mean a lot more than just money in your bank account.

MAKE YOUR LIFE COUNT!

GET GREAT

"But be not afraid of Greatness:
Some are born Great,
some achieve Greatness,
and some have Greatness thrust upon them."
— William Shakespeare

You have four levels of Greatness.

- ❖ Potential Greatness means you can be great.
- ❖ Possible Greatness means you may be great.
- ❖ Probable Greatness means on your way to being great.
- ❖ Present Greatness means you are great.

You must go from "you can be great" to "you are great."

In a one-on-one interview with Michael Jordan regarding the first fifty years of his life, Ahmad Rashad asked him if fear of failure was a motivator. Michael Jordan's answer was:

"I never feared about my skills because I put in the work. Work ethic eliminates fear; if you put in the work, then what are you fearing? You know what you are capable of and what you are not. Limits like fears are often just an illusion."

Remove the limitations you have placed on yourself by dedicating yourself to "Mastery." Do it for those who love you, do it for those you love.

Get great!

LIVING LEGACY

"Success is not Success, without a Successor"
— Deion Sanders

(aka Coach Prime)

When you reminisce about the glory days of yesteryear and you are ready to ride off blissfully into the sunset, how will you have prepared for that moment?

The great Zig Ziglar once said, "You must gather your fruit in the valley for the mountain top."

That fruit, Beloved, is what you will leave behind. Never take solace in settling; attain or die exhausted in the endeavor.

Most say leave a legacy, but I say live a legacy. In his book, Instinct, TD Jakes wrote, *"Recognize the adequacy of what is within you to survive and succeed amid all you face. You do have what it takes to master the outward challenges as you release your inner resources."*[35]

Living your Legacy means people can see your impact in action (while you are still here). Therefore, I encourage you to always remember: Be your best because life is too short to be anything less.

LEAD TO SUCCEED

"You can be a leader without being an entrepreneur,
but you cannot be an entrepreneur without being a leader."
— Roger Daye

---

[35] Jakes, T.D. Instinct, The Power to Unleash Your Inborn Drive. (Nashville: FaithWords, a division of Hatchette Book Group, Inc.; 2015); page 262

Leaders don't always have to make entrepreneurial decisions. But entrepreneurs always have to make leadership decisions.

You are a Leader!

What is the difference between good leadership and great leadership? Good leadership gets the most out of people, whereas great leadership gets the best out of people. Why does that matter? Getting the most out of people means they give you all they can. Getting the best out of people means they grow to give more.

Good leadership is solid leadership, whereas great leadership is servant leadership.

"Yet it shall not be so among you; but whoever desires to become great among you shall be your servant. And whoever of you desires to be first shall be slave of all. For even the Son of Man did not come to be served, but to serve, and to give His life a ransom for many."
— **Mark 10:43-45 (NKJV)**

Jesus Christ modeled Servant Leadership as the blueprint for us to follow as leaders.

Dr. Myles Munroe who said, "Trapped in every follower is a leader... It is mentality, not ability, that makes you a leader."

As a leader, you must understand that your viability is predicated upon the experience, effectiveness, and efficiency of those whom you lead. (Even if it is just you by yourself for now.)

Therefore, you must leverage your energy and expertise to equip a team that will become an extension of you.

*"Leaders who attract followers... impact only people they touch.
Leaders who develop leaders... impact people beyond their reach."*

— **John Maxwell**

CAN WE WORK TOGETHER?

Working as a team can make the impossible—possible,
but working on your own can make the possible; impossible.
— **Dr. Lewis T. Kola**
(Licensed Professional Counselor, DMin, LPC, LMFT, MAC)

No great sports team is a success without a great coach. I welcome the opportunity to help you fulfill your potential. When I ask the question, "Can we work together?" The emphasis would be on "WE."

You see, I believe:

Personal GROWTH will lead to professional and profitable GROWTH.

Therefore, I am committed to doing my job, which is to help you grow. I need you to be committed to doing your job, which is to grow what you do.

"Grow You, then Grow what You Do!"

How to GROW You:

1. Ask God for the Wisdom (James 1:5-9).
2. Ask God for the Way (Hebrews 12:1-2; Proverbs 4:14-15).
3. Ask God for the Will to do the Work (Philippians 2:13).

To unlock your full potential, you must take purposeful action to grow yourself personally, professionally, and profitably.

*I will help **YOU** build your business!*

Now, while that may look like one statement, there are really two promises being made:

- ❖ Promise #1: I will help *YOU*
- ❖ Promise #2: *YOU* build your business

INSPIRATION IS ALWAYS BETTER THAN MOTIVATION

To inspire means to do the work from the inside out. Inspiration gives people an internal driver for external accomplishments, but the push to get it done comes from a powerful place within the individual.

Motivation, on the other hand, begins from an external source, meaning you must have a motive for action to go forward as opposed to an internal push.

Which do you think is easier, pushing or pulling? Let me put it like this; if a car runs out of gas would you rather push it or pull it to the gas station? Inspiration is a push from within whereas Motivation is a pulling from without.

Both are powerful means to move a person forward but the best way to get a person to start moving in the right direction begins with Inspiration.

With this book my hope was to inspire you to take action and build a better life. If you need further assistance, please visit **www.mpower-me.info** and go to the "Contact Us" page to schedule a consultation.

THE MPOWER SUCCESS SYSTEM

My dream for MPOWER is that we are a company that strives to assist people who are willing to achieve all that is within them through a process that leads to prosperity and the fulfillment of their purpose.

MPOWER is a Biblically based, scripturally sound success system that is designed to help people pursue a purposeful path in life, leadership, and legacy.

We achieve this aim by focusing on three areas of growth:

- ❖ Personal Excellence
- ❖ Professional Expertise
- ❖ Profitable Execution.

This is done by concentrating on three core components:

- ❖ Elevate your Mind
- ❖ Educate yourself on Methods
- ❖ Evaluate your Model.

Therefore, we place an emphasis on three points of responsibility, which are:

- ❖ Mastery of your Mentality.
- ❖ Mastery of your Methodology.
- ❖ Mastery of your Modality.

It is this systematic approach that delivers on our promise to help a person become a high achiever. Our goal is to see people realize their endeavors through progressive accomplishment.

To learn more, please visit www.mpowersuccesssystem.com.

MY FINAL THOUGHT

I want to leave you with this: I give all Glory, Honor, and Praise to God for His Grace and Goodness, which allowed me to complete this very tall task.

The greatest challenge to my completing this book was my self-sabotaging behaviors and self-imposed limitations. I had both a fear of failure and a fear of success.

Yes, the "Success Coach" was afraid of success.

Writing this book has tested me in more ways than I care to count, but the person who started this project is not the same person who finished it (Rom 8:28).

It was inevitable that I would be different when I embarked on this journey of continuous improvement.

Whenever you set out to do anything greater than you, you go through stages of growth.

Here are the three things that I realized above all else:

- ❖ Self-Discovery, meaning I will never reach myself.
- ❖ Self-Development, meaning I will never beat myself.
- ❖ Self-Dedication, meaning I will never cheat myself.

This is the power of transformation; a metamorphosis must take place. Metamorphosis means a manifestation of change that is proven by results. What results do you want to see manifested in your life? You now know what it takes to achieve those results. Use the "Combination of Success" to unlock success in your life.

NOW WHAT?

Now that you have completed this book, what do you do?

My hope was this book would be a place for you to pivot and course correct. If it felt like an information overload, this was done purposely because my goal was to overdeliver.

With that in mind, go to **www.mpower-me.info** for your next steps.

MPOWER ME

About The Author

Roger L. Daye was born and raised in Durham, NC, but currently resides in Atlanta, Georgia.

He is an Author, Speaker, and Certified Success Coach to help you in the areas of Life, Leadership, and Legacy.

He emphasizes personal growth through teaching, inspirational speaking, one-on-one, and group coaching.

His expertise is in helping people realize their own potential through his "Combination to Success."

Roger is the Founder of MPOWER Development Group, which offers Coaching, Consulting, and a Course Curriculum.

Mastery
PO**M**ER
People Overcome with Education & Resources

Roger focuses on building strengths through self-discovery, detailed action plans, and his proven personal development program, the "MPOWER Success System." His practical yet unique style has compelled numerous individuals to change for the better and achieve their goals.

He has one singular desire to help people focus forward by going God-ward to get them to their "Place of Destiny."

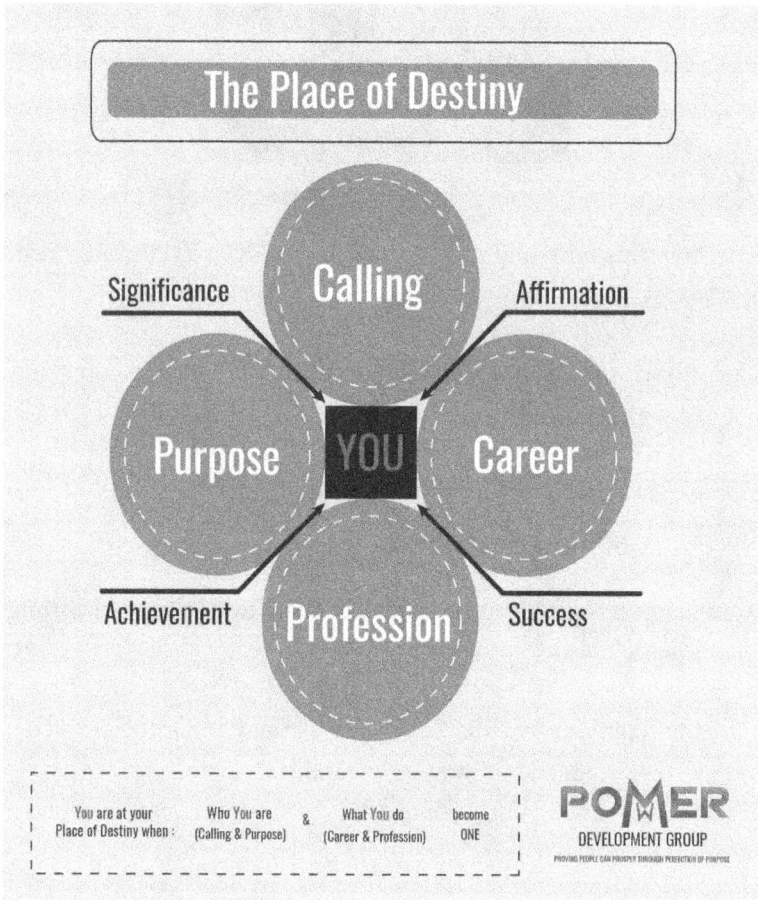

The Place of Destiny

Significance   Calling   Affirmation

Purpose   YOU   Career

Achievement   Profession   Success

You are at your Place of Destiny when: Who You are (Calling & Purpose) & What You do (Career & Profession) become ONE

PO**M**ER DEVELOPMENT GROUP
PROVING PEOPLE CAN PROSPER THROUGH PERFECTION OF PURPOSE

Bibliography

1 Eker, T. Harv. *Secrets of the Millionaire Mind* (New York City: HarperCollins Publishers, 2009), p. 9.

2 Robbins, Tony. *Business Thought. Profit Magazine, 2008.* www.profitmagazin.com/editions/number_061.481.html

3 Westacott, Emrys. "What Is a Paradigm Shift?" *ThoughtCo*, January 22, 2019, www.thoughtco.com/what-is-a-paradigm-shift-2670671

4 Robbins, Tony. *The 3 Steps to a Breakthrough. 2015,* https://www.tonyrobbins.com/podcasts/3-steps-breakthrough/

5 Siegel, Daniel J. *The Developing Mind* (New York: The Guilford Press, 2012), pp. 210-211.

6 Hill, Napoleon. *Think and Grow Rich* (New York: Skyhorse, 2016), p. 19.

7 Wiskup, Mark. *The It Factor and How to Get It: Becoming a Master Communicator, 2019.* www.amanet.org/training/webcasts/the-it-factor-and-how-to-get-it-becoming-a-master-communicator.aspx

8 Wattles, Wallace. *The Science of Getting Rich. Abridged Edition* (Pennsylvania: Tremendous Life Books), p. 10.

9 Maxwell, John. *The Power of Attitude* (Illinois: David C. Cook, 2001).

10 Borden, Kit. "What is the difference between altitude and attitude in aeronautics?" *Quora*, January 29, 2018. www.quora.com/What-is-the-difference-between-altitude-and-attitude-in-aeronautics

[11] Zimmerman, *Alan. Pivot: How One Change in Attitude Can Lead to Success* (United Kingdom: Peak Performance Publishers), p. 2.

[12] Maxwell, John. *Attitude 101: What Every Leader Needs to Know* (New York City: HarperCollins Publishers, LLC, 2003), p. 4.

[13] Helmenstine, Ph.D., Anne Marie. Last accessed 2018. https://www.thoughtco.com/definition-of-scientific-law-605643

[14] *The Science of Personality. Psychology Today.* Last Accessed 2018. https://www.psychologytoday.com/us/basics/personality

[15] Maxwell, John. *The 15 Invaluable Laws of Growth* (New York City: Center Street, a division of Hachette Book Group, Inc., 2014), p. 9.

[16] Hill, Napoleon. *Think and Grow Rich* (New York: Skyhorse; 2016), p. 19.

[17] *History of the Secret.* Last accessed 2018; https://www.thesecret.tv/about/history-of-the-secret/

[18] Shakespeare, William. *Hamlet.* (New York City: Simon & Schuster Paperbacks, 2003), p. 127.

[19] Covey, Stephen. *The 7 Habits of Highly Effective People* (New York City: Simon & Schuster, 2013), p. 102.

[20] Hill, Napoleon. *What the Mind Can Conceive,* Believe & *Achieve.* October 19, 2007. https://www.youtube.com/watch?v=2hA-7aq6OXI

[21] Sinclair, Seth. "How Do Adults Learn?" Last accessed 2018, http://sinclairadvisorygroup.blogspot.com/2014/11/how-do-adults-learn-why-does-it-matter.html

[22] Mind. *Wikipedia.* Last accessed 2018. https://en.wikipedia.org/wiki/Mind

[23] Dweck, Carol. *Mindset: The New Psychology of Success* (New York City: Ballantine Books, a division of Penguin Random House LLC, 2007), pp. 6-9.

[24] Canfield, Jack. *The Success Principles: How to get from Where You Are to Where You Want to Be* (New York City: HarperCollins Publishers; 2015), pp. 6-7.

[25] "A Walk Through the Human Mind." Last accessed 2018. http://www.ascend25d.com/index.php/2016/04/27/a-walk-through-the-human-mind/

[26] Bradberry, Travis. "Why You Need Emotional Intelligence to Succeed." *Success Magazine,* January 25, 2016: www.success.com/article/why-you-need-emotional-intelligence-to-succeed

[27] Wattles, Wallace. *The Science of Getting Rich, Abridged Edition.* (Pennsylvania: Tremendous Life Books), p. 11.

[28] Olsen, Jeff. *The Slight Edge: Turning Simple Disciplines into Massive Success and Happiness* (Austin: Greenleaf Book Group Press, 2013), p. 58.

[29] Cardone, Grant. *The 10X Rule: The Only Difference Between Success and Failure* (Hoboken: John Wiley & Sons, Inc., 2013), pp. 40-43.

[30] Fabrega, Marelisa. "The Key To Goal Success: Setting Implementation Intentions." 2013. https://daringtolivefully.com/implementation-intentions

[31] Cognitive Dissonance. WikiQuote. Last accessed 2018. https://en.wikiquote.org/wiki/Cognitive_dissonance.

[32] Canfield, Jack. *The Success Principles: How to get from Where You Are to Where You Want to Be* (New York City: HarperCollins Publishers; 2015), p. 147.

[33] Hults, Donald. *Unseen Untold is Unsold: Salesmanship & Common Sense* (Indiana: Trafford Publishing, 2009), p. 44.

[34] Canfield, Jack, and Hansen, Mark Victor. *The* Aladdin *Factor* (New York City: Berkeley Books Publishers, 1995).

[35] Jakes, T.D. Instinct, The Power to Unleash Your Inborn Drive. (Nashville: FaithWords, a division of Hachette Book Group, Inc., 2015), p. 262.

THANK YOU FOR READING MY BOOK!

Just to say Thank You, I would like to give you a Free Gift!

Scan the QR Code:

I appreciate your interest in my book and value your feedback, as it helps me improve future versions. I would appreciate it if you could leave your invaluable review on Amazon.com with your feedback. Thank you!

www.ingramcontent.com/pod-product-compliance
Lightning Source LLC
Chambersburg PA
CBHW050503210326
41521CB00011B/2303